In the
SHADOW
of
MERCURY

A MEMOIR OF MID-LIFE AND DOGS

In the
SHADOW
of
MERCURY

A MEMOIR OF MID-LIFE AND DOGS

MELANIE CORONETZ

To order additional copies of this book, contact:
Xlibris Corporation
1-888-795-4274
www.Xlibris.com
Orders@Xlibris.com
44898

Contents

For all the dogs who brought both joy and heartache into my life—

Rusty, Dobie, Mercury, Eva, Monkey, Argo, Lucy, Marlena, Mozart

. . . and Vivi

My little dog—a heartbeat at my feet.

Edith Wharton

With very special thanks to Lynne Lancaster and Wendy Levine, whose input and critical eyes made this book possible.

Chapter 1

My Dazzling Careers

In 1984, on my fortieth birthday, my husband Bruce took a picture of me in our living room. I was wearing a silver unitard, and the camera flash made it glint like polished steel. I made a copy of that photo and sent it to my brother in Seattle. I wanted him to see his older sis looking as sleek and shiny as a barracuda, just like the one he saw up close on one of his scuba diving trips to warm waters. Maybe prancing around the living room in that stretchy jumpsuit was a sign that ordinary middle age wasn't for me. I'd soon quit my job, try new careers, and follow a path that eventually led to a little black dog I'd name Mercury.

Two years after that big birthday, I left the ad agency where I worked as a copywriter. My small, friendly agency had merged with a bigger firm, one that employed a nasty receptionist who had a sign-in sheet on her desk to identify people arriving after 9:00. To me, this was an outrage. Writers and other creative types never had had to conform to strict rules at the old agency. I'd usually arrive by 9:30 and no one would snarl, not even my boss. Another thing wrong with this mega-agency was its location at Dag Hammarskjold Plaza, near the U.N. Apart from trying to pronounce or spell it, Dag Plaza was a wasteland. If I didn't have a client lunch at one of the nearby expense account restaurants, there was nothing to do at mid-day. That's why I'd always chosen the companies I worked for by their proximity to Fifth Avenue, the street where I lived, about a mile uptown. In a pinch, or a transit strike, I could walk home. Easy commutes on the Lexington Avenue subway or the Fifth Avenue bus were essential to my well-being. I could read my newspaper or a book. I could get off at my stop and arrive at my office without trekking half way across town. As most people living in the city know, and as most visitors soon find out, Manhattan crosstown streets are much longer than blocks going north and south. In fact, any company too far from Fifth Avenue for a visit to Saks at lunchtime was off my list, even if the opportunity was great and the pay was better. That's why Dag, on Second Avenue, didn't cut it.

My boss was stunned when I asked him to fire me. I supposed no one had ever put him on the spot like that. His expression softened, though, when I said I'd lined up a replacement, an eager young woman from Queens who clearly was more interested in building a career than working near first class shopping. The day I left the agency, I walked home. It took forever, and that put to rest any doubts I may have had that a Second Avenue location was akin to Siberia.

I'd planned my quitting to coincide with summer, a time when softened asphalt can suck a Manolo right off one's foot. Bruce and I had rented a house on Shelter Island, a small land mass tucked between the two forks of eastern Long Island. Back then, in the early 1980s, it was a quiet spot without pretension or croissants. A night out could mean a dance at the school, or a chicken barbecue under a community tent. The house we chose was as quirky as we were. It had been constructed from the outbuildings of an estate. The long living room was once a tea dance pavillion, and the upstairs bedroom sat in a tower which had been moved from its original perch overlooking the bay. While we couldn't see the water, because another house blocked the view, the beach was a short walk down a skinny dirt path on the side of the neighboring property. Bruce planned to come out on weekends, and I'd stay at the house to enjoy summery activities—tennis, swimming, and being lazy. This was a perfect place to launch a new career—as a painter.

I'd never seriously studied art except for a required Fine Arts course in college. As a child, like most kids of that era, I'd made my share of "paint by numbers" masterpieces. I recall one vividly, a tiger set amidst vibrant green plants in a jungle. I remember selecting the paints, each tube numbered to correspond to a pre-marked area in the painting. When my tiger was finished, I was disappointed that my folks never framed it or hung it with pride in the living room.

Now I had another chance to let that inner artist erupt. This time, instead of oils, I bought a set of watercolor paints and an instruction book, plus water color paper. I didn't want the mess of cleaning brushes with turpentine or the expense of buying canvasses. I pictured myself gathering flowers from the garden, installing them in a vase and creating lovely still lifes that people would admire. But I had no talent. After copying a few pictures from the book, then trying other subjects on my own, I produced results that only a mother could love—but not hang. It was clear that "artist" was not going to be my mid-life career.

Summer passed and I returned to the city. Through an art director friend I knew from the pre-merger days of the small ad agency, I picked up a few freelance copywriting assignments. This meant working for mom and pop businesses, one-man or woman start-ups, and small companies too cheap to hire a real advertising agency. It meant eating sandwiches off a plastic tray instead of enjoying a leisurely lunch at a white table cloth restaurant. It also meant traveling to parts of the city I never would have considered as a home base when I worked as an employee. But worst of all, I soon discovered the biggest challenge of freelancing: Getting paid. Clients, or at least the ones I had, paid their dog-sitters way before they ever thought of paying me. Though this was ego-bruising, it wasn't life threatening. My husband worked on Wall Street and cheerfully took care of the bills, though later, as I kept trying but not succeeding at finding a suitable new career, he began to grumble. As for my clients, they seemed to forget I wasn't a volunteer. I expected to get paid for my efforts. In one case, I sued a dead beat in small claims court after months of cajoling him to pay the pittance I'd billed him. It took more time than it was worth. First, there was the forty minute subway ride downtown to the dingy courthouse. Perhaps it's been redecorated by now, but back then, the crowded room with its grayish green walls and bare bulb lighting made me wonder if I'd wandered into a holding pen for law breakers. I remember waiting on a line to find out which forms I needed, then rifling through an unkempt rack until I found them. I filled them out, stood on another slow-moving line to pay the fee and turn them in, and left, hoping I'd at least get some money back. After a few months, I received notice that I won the case and the client, now ex-client, eventually paid. Freelancing, I concluded, had too many headaches and none of the benefits of a satisfying mid-life pastime.

We rented the same house the following summer. Its quiet location, at the end of a private road marked "Lands End," provided the perfect place for me to finish my secret project—writing a romance novel. In fact, this wasn't my first novel. It was my third. I'd written number one with my client when I was still at the small agency. She worked for a travel company that specialized in trips for older people, and she had traveled pretty much everywhere in the world. Her experiences provided the background and authentic notes we needed to make our book intriguing. We used to arrange business meetings at the end of the day, then I'd stay at her office and we'd work out a plan for a chapter. We'd each go home and write. She'd do a chapter and I'd craft the next one. Our writing styles were similar, so it seemed, at least to us, that one person, not two, was at the helm of this great masterpiece. In a week or two, we'd schedule another business meeting, followed by another work session for our novel. I'm sure my boss at the agency was pleased that I was giving this important client so much attention.

It took us a good six months to write our novel, and when it was finished we were deliriously pleased with the result. We even made up a pseudonym, using parts of our first and last names. Pamela Lynetz. Didn't that have a snappy ring? After our book had been rejected, with a cruel letter of dismissal from the agent who'd agreed to read it, I decided to write one on my own. I didn't tell my client. I was sure I could do better. The one I wrote with her took place in the jungles of Indonesia. It had an exotic setting and handsome characters, but the romance was tepid and the plot, though I don't remember it, must've stunk. When I look back, I have no qualms about having put my copy of the manuscript into the shredder.

Back in the early 1970s, a good decade before I arrived at this mid-point in my life, I'd worked on Wall Street. No, I wasn't a trader or a stock broker. I was a receptionist. I sat behind a huge antique desk, in a large wood paneled room. Oil paintings of the firm's founding fathers hung on the walls. Their unsmiling faces seemed to say that I'd better not make a mistake or I'd be out the door. It was a solemn, formal atmosphere, one that I drew upon when I wrote my own romance novel, *Wall Street Lover* that summer on Shelter Island. It was also a parking place and rent payer until I could finish my Masters degree in French literature and find a teaching job at a university. I had spent a year in Paris after graduating from college. When I returned home, I found a position teaching French at a junior high on Long Island. It was a two-year assignment, filling in for someone on maternity leave, and when she came back, I was out of a job. I didn't mind. I had discovered I wasn't a very good teacher. I liked the smart kids, but had little patience for the slower students. The year I received my M.A., the placement office posted one opening for a French professor—at a junior college in Arizona. I didn't apply.

Shortly after receiving that degree, I went to grad school for another, an M.B.A. It was at Pace, not Harvard, and that was just as well. I wasn't at ease with numbers or mind-challenging financial concepts. To this day, I remember the accounting teacher, turning red in the face, losing his cool, and crying out, "Why can't you understand?"

By sheer good luck, I landed at the McCall Pattern Company. It wasn't sewing skills that got me there. It was my French. They needed someone to help screen applicants to translate sewing patterns into French to comply with Canada's newly enacted bilingual laws. Did I mention that McCall's was just a short walk to Saks?

Four years later, when McCall's was sold, I tried yet another career, in advertising. I started as an account executive, thanks to my M.B.A., but after a few years, I switched to copywriting in direct response, a.k.a. junk mail. I had a knack for writing letters. When I eventually ended up at the small agency where I met the client who wrote that first novel with me, I became known as the Queen of Letters.

Looking back, I don't regret floundering around, looking for the right career fit. The receptionist job, as I mentioned, provided authentic background for *Wall Street Lover*. I even found an agent, a woman who, I'm sure, had never met the first agent, otherwise she would have run the other way. To her credit, she tried to sell this book. She sent it out, and it came back, then she sent it out again. After a year, with a pile of rejection slips as thick as today's Shelter Island phone book, it was becoming clear that I didn't have a knack for writing romance novels. But I enjoyed writing. While *Wall Street Lover* was getting the ping pong treatment, I wrote my third and last fiction book: *In the Lobsterman's Trap*. If nothing else, I came up with good titles. Too bad the stories didn't measure up.

Suddenly, my dilettante days came to an abrupt end. In October 1987, the stock market crashed and dozens of firms went out of business. The one where my husband worked was among them. It didn't shut down right away, but withered to a close a few months later. I took a job to help pay expenses. This time I was a secretary, and the man I worked for, a lawyer in a non-profit organization, was a pompous ass. He had no sense of humor and never cracked a smile. He could've been part of the stone-faced gang hanging in the main office at the Wall Street firm. I dreaded going to work. But now, I couldn't go back to advertising because all the small agencies, the kind I enjoyed working in, had merged with bigger ones. I didn't like teaching. In fact, I realized I didn't like business. Fortunately, we had no children, and at the time, no dogs, so there were no extra mouths to feed, no vet bills to take care of, or private school tuitions to pay. That year, it was a lean Christmas.

Over the years, Bruce and I had talked about getting a dog. Friends of ours had a fun-loving Golden Retriever named Buster, and each time we visited them, we yearned for a furry pal of our own. Buster could understand French, or so it seemed. When Carolyn, his "mom," said, "fromage," Buster licked his lips. Then she'd place a piece of cheese on his nose. He wouldn't eat it until she said, "mangez." Then he'd flip the cheese off his nose right into his mouth. I pictured myself spending many happy days with my own dog, teaching him or her tricks, speaking French and entertaining our friends. What better use for a Masters degree, than for training a dog?

Chapter 2

Rusty, Maxie and Dobie

Both Bruce and I had dogs when we were kids. Rusty, a Cocker Spaniel, was my buddy when I was in elementary school. She'd come from a pet shop, of course, because that's where people bought dogs back then. No one knew about breeders, nor did they know much about dog training. Unfortunately for Rusty, my parents believed in the "stick the dog's face in the mess and that's how she'll learn" technique. They also disciplined her by swatting her with rolled up newspapers. Despite that abuse, Rusty remained a sweet dog with a friendly personality. I have vague memories of her kissing my nose and lying on her back to have her belly scratched. Rusty also had that special Cocker Spaniel way of handling excitement—peeing on the floor—even if she'd been out just a short time before. When company came, we tried to have her greet them in the yard.

My parents had given Rusty to me after my brother and sister were born. My mom took care of the babies, and I, seven years older than those crying critters, took care of Rusty. I loved her. That's why it broke my heart when I came home from school one day, ready to take her for her afternoon walk, to find out that she'd run away. I remember walking the streets of our town, every afternoon for two weeks, crying and calling her name. I never found her, and it was only much later in life that I learned the truth. Rusty had picked up a tick which had burrowed deep into her ear canal. By the time my parents noticed something wrong and took her to the veterinarian, she had developed an infection that couldn't be cured. They had her put down and mistakenly thought they were somehow protecting me by saying she'd run off.

Maxie, a mutt, grew up in my husband's family. She came from the pound, the old time name for an animal shelter. To this day, Bruce and his brothers talk of Maxie's intelligence. I'm not sure how they did it, but they trained her to go down into the basement where her food was stored, and bring up a can of meat for her dinner. Today, she'd probably be a television star.

Dobie came to us in another way one shouldn't acquire a dog. A family friend, who also was my brother's second grade teacher, gave him to us as a surprise. No one knew what this little dog was. He looked like a Doberman Pinscher, but pint sized, and that's what we called him whenever anyone asked—a miniature Doberman. We had never heard of Min Pins. Dobie the "Doberman," Rusty the reddish hued Cocker. We sure had a knack for coming up with original names.

Today, when breeders talk about big dogs in small bodies, I always think of Dobie. In the 1960s, my family had a beach house in the Springs, an area about 8 miles outside the village of East Hampton on Long Island. Deer, pheasant, turtles and raccoons thrived in that pre-development era. One day a herd of deer dared to meander across our beach. Dobie saw them before any of us did. He plunged down the stairs leading to the beach and scared the deer into the bay. What a crazy dog, I thought. But in the next second, I witnessed an even crazier action. Dobie had jumped into the water and was swimming after the deer, chasing them further and further away from the shore. I panicked. I imagined my little pal getting tired and sinking. I called him, but he was fixated on the deer. It was early autumn and the water was still warm enough for humans to swim in it comfortably. I ran back upstairs and put on a bathing suit, then dove into the bay to follow Dobie. I finally got his attention, and I suspect he was glad I'd come after him. I held him under his belly so he could "swim" on his own back to shore.

I was away at college when Dobie reached his sixteenth year. He'd lost a good part of his eyesight, and his legs weren't as strong as they'd been in his deer chasing days. He was having accidents in the house. I don't know exactly when my parents decided to put him down, but when they did, they let me know via a long distance phone call. They buried him in the front yard at the beach house. It's been over twenty-five years since they sold the house and moved away, but one of my friend's mothers still lives in that area. Whenever my friend comes down from Connecticut to visit her mom in the summer, I drive over from Shelter Island and pass our old house. Trees have grown thick in the front yard and have obscured most of the property. I can no longer see Dobie's grave, but as I go by, I silently call his name.

Chapter 3

Nug

It's my belief that every generation learns from the previous one's missteps. For my husband and me, this was especially true with regard to dogs. We had no intention of getting a dog from a pet shop, and we told our closest friends and relatives not to put a pup in our Christmas stocking. We considered a dog from a shelter, but what we really wanted was a Bull Terrier. Ever since the movie, *Patton,* which we'd seen independently since we didn't know each other at the time, we were intrigued by this breed. We thought they were peculiar looking, in an interesting way, and we nicknamed them "nugly dogs," a take-off on "ugly." Now, if any Bull Terrier people are reading this, they'll probably barrage me with nasty emails, but to them I say, "Wait. Let me explain." Both Bruce and I were, and still are, off-beat and somewhat eccentric. For example, the only time we turn on the television is to watch football (his choice) and tennis, which we both like. We have no children because we never wanted any, and we married late, in our forties, after living together for twelve years. For people born in the 1940s, just before the baby boom, this was considered unconventional, even bizarre, behavior.

That Christmas, I gave Bruce a Bull Terrier. I'd made it myself, out of *papier mâché,* working in the kitchen of our apartment during the day, while he was at work. I'd quit the stuffy lawyer months before, the moment Bruce found a new job. Now I was free, once again, to dabble and try new things. I had once made a horse out of *papier mâché* in art class when I was in grade school. I remember mixing flour and water in a bowl to form the paste, and tearing old newspapers into strips. If

I could make a horse, I could make a dog. I started accumulating my materials. One of Bruce's weird hobbies was collecting old newspapers and clipping out articles that interested him. He'd stack them in a pile in his den, with the intention, I suppose, of reading them one day. This was a veritable warehouse of supplies for my project, so tempting, yet so forbidden. If I'd removed even a year-old sports section, somehow, he'd know it was missing. I had to find another source, and I did, in the basement of our building. I took other people's discarded newspapers, and within a week, I had the makings of my "nugly dog."

At night, I hid the body in my closet. By day, I added more paste-laden strips to the frame. Little by little, "Nug," took shape. Since I wasn't gifted in art—remember those watercolor attempts?—it surprised me that my creation really did resemble a Bull Terrier. The more strips I added, the more muscled "Nug" became. After a few weeks, when he was thoroughly dry, I painted him white, glued on buttons for eyes, and encircled one with a black patch. By the way, this was just before Target and Spuds MacKenzie made Bull Terriers famous. As a finishing touch, I bought a red bandanna and tied it around his neck. Bruce was thrilled with his gift.

"Nug" was a dry run for a real live dog. After dinner, for example, we'd have dog-centered pseudo arguments. "Your turn to take him out," my husband might say.

"No, it's your turn. I took him out last night." We'd flip a coin and the loser would put on his or her coat, go out in the hall with "Nug", and return about 15 minutes later, the right amount of time for a quick evening walk. In the morning, I always took "Nug" out. Back then, I liked to jog, and since we lived across the street from Central Park, one of the most dog friendly places in the city, I had the perfect location. While I didn't actually take "Nug" with me on these jaunts, I imagined a real Bull Terrier, trundling along beside me as I circumnavigated the bridle path that went around the reservoir.

That summer, buoyed by my success at creating a realistic dog out of *papier mâché*, I decided to make more Bull Terriers and sell them. We had, by then, bought our own place on Shelter Island, an old house from the early 1850s with two acres of land. On the lawn, in bright sunlight, I pictured an entire kennel drying in a week. I made four bodies, rolling the newspaper and folding it, to form the skeletons, then adding crumpled balls which I covered with the wetted strips. But the dogs didn't dry fast enough to accommodate the layers of wet newspaper, and in the end, all their backs caved in. Maybe I should've marketed them as sway backed old nags. A friend of mine owned a shop down the road, and I placed them there on consignment. By the end of the summer, not one had sold. Perhaps it was the price—$40 apiece—or perhaps people couldn't see the connection between my dogs and the newly popular Spuds MacKenzie. I took them all back and eventually gave them away, free to good homes.

Bruce is not a talkative man when it comes to relationships. He never expressed his dismay at my inability to make money. But I knew it was there. I could sense it, especially with the romance novels, which often elicited snide remarks from him and nothing in the way of encouragement. He might've been happier marrying another investment banker, or a stock analyst, someone who could talk business and who knew all the players on Wall Street. Instead he got me. I suppose I misled him in a way, by getting that M.B.A. and having some good jobs at the outset. He probably thought I'd rise up the career ladder, giving us a healthy dual income and a circle of like-minded friends. But I fooled him. Not deliberately, of course. But I fooled him. Now I had another flop to add to my resume, *papier mâché* dogs. By then, I was a few years short of fifty, and other women I knew, especially those with M.B.A.s were toodling along in their careers, enjoying success, and buying Manolos and cars with their own money, not their husband's. I felt like a second class citizen. Perhaps I should have been more focused after I'd come home from my graduate year in Paris.

Interspersed with these ventures that didn't pan out, I did have one stretch of glory—with horses. In my thirties and forties, I'd done a lot of riding, sometimes in Central Park, but mostly in Westchester and Orange County, New York. I did a bit of foxhunting, though, happily, we never saw a fox. I also did some hunter paces, galloping cross country and popping over stone walls and ditches. It was exhilarating and fun, plus it afforded new shopping opportunities. A rider needed boots, breeches, a hard hat, hunt coat and the proper accessories. At that time, in New York, there were two wonderful stores that sold riding gear, Knoud's and Miller's. I loved visiting them, sniffing the aroma of leather given off by the boots and tack for sale. I didn't have my own horse, but aside from that, I was totally horsey. Since I'd worked writing copy, a logical step, I thought, was writing features for horse magazines. For once I was right. When I queried both *Practical Horseman* and *Horseplay* with ideas for articles, they were interested, and subsequently each accepted my work. Plus they paid for it.

As the Bull Terrier summer was coming to a close, my husband discovered a pea-sized lump in one of his testicles. It turned out to be cancer, and he had to have surgery, followed by an intense course of chemo. This required hospital stays. I was sure he was going to die. He must've been frightened, too, because he refused to talk about his illness. This made me feel totally alone and useless. At the outset, friends asked about him, but after a while, when I couldn't tell them anything new, they stopped asking. I became depressed. Bruce had shut me out. Friends returned to living their own lives. At that point, I must admit, I didn't much care what happened to me, so I decided to take a job as a bicycle messenger. I pictured myself zooming though traffic, wearing spandex and scaring pedestrians. If I got squashed by a bus, so much the better.

My husband still went to work, except for the days he had chemo. He lost his hair, and he continued his campaign of silence. For many couples, a serious illness brings a new closeness in a marriage. In our case, it drove us further apart. He couldn't talk to me, and after a while, I gave up trying to talk to him. It became clear, if we were going to stay together, that we needed marriage counseling or a dog, perhaps both.

I began researching Bull Terriers. I visited the library at the American Kennel Club and read books on Bullies. I spoke with breeders. In fact, I did all the legwork one was supposed to do to make an informed decision before purchasing a dog. In the end, I decided, the Bull Terrier wasn't for us. Besides some health problems in the breed, the males could weigh up to 75 pounds and the females, 45. This was too much dog for me. I couldn't imagine trying to get such a dog in and out of its crate in the car when we went to the country. I took out the phone book and began to make a list of messenger services.

One afternoon, not too long after I had decided to become a messenger, I turned on the television and surfed the dial. Though I rarely watched tv, I don't know what made me tune in that day. It must've been fate. One of the stations was showing a replay of the previous year's Westminster Kennel Club Dog Show. Just at the moment I caught it, a handler was showing a breed of small dog in the non-sporting group. I listened to the announcer. "Schipperke," he said, as he proceeded to give background information on this Belgian breed. I had never heard of Schipperkes before, but I loved what I saw—a small black dog that resembled a fox without a tail. This was a dog I could pick up and put in the car. This was a dog that maybe, just maybe, was perfect for us.

Chapter 4

Mercury Rising

Off I went, once again, to the AKC library. There I found a small collection of old books and magazine articles. I learned that the ancestors of the Schipperke were first seen on farms during the middle ages, in the Flanders region of what today is Belgium. Of course, it looked nothing like dogs we know today. This distant relative, the Leuvenaar, was slightly taller and a bit shaggier. It also had no tail. Today, it is extinct. The actual history of the breed began in 1690, in Brussels. Members of the Shoemaker's Guild used to organize competitions on Sundays to show off their dogs. Each one sported a handmade brass collar, crafted by its owner, which naturally led to rivalries and attempts at one-upsmanship. Schipperkes became the official mascots of the Shoemaker's Guild, which helped create the myth of how the breed became tailless. According to legend, a shoemaker, annoyed that another man's Schipperke was trespassing on his property, perhaps in search of some juicy leather shoes to munch on, caught the dog and chopped off its tail. Afterwards, everyone thought the animal looked better without this appendage, and the tailless Schipperke became the norm. Today, most people think of Schipperkes as the companions of the boatmen whose barges cruised the canals. The little black dogs were fierce rat catchers and highly vocal watchdogs. Later in the 1880s, Queen Marie-Henriette of Belgium took a shine to the breed and they became popular pets.

Schipperkes, I learned, have an independent streak. They are clever and curious, always wanting to know, for example, what's behind that closed door, or in that shopping bag left on the floor. The males weigh about 18 pounds and the females 12 to 16. Their coat pattern is natural, so they don't have to go to the groomer's for expensive clipping. I asked the librarian to make copies of some of the articles so I could show Bruce. But this was merely a courtesy. I had found my breed.

Shortly afterwards, I saw an ad in *The New York Times,* Schipperke puppies for sale. The breeder lived in Bedford, an upscale Westchester village, and it was an easy drive straight up Route 684. However, I knew from my Bull Terrier research that buying a dog through a newspaper wasn't always a good idea. The breeder could be, for example, someone just mating dogs to produce puppies to make money or to show children the "miracle of birth." He or she might not know, or care, about examining pedigrees to ensure that health problems didn't get passed on. Knowing the pitfalls in advance gave me the confidence to answer the ad. At the very least, I could see the pups, then decide.

We made an appointment for the following weekend. It was a mild day in early March and the drive to Bedford went quickly. There was no snow on the ground, and very little traffic. I had bought a puppy-sized collar and lead, plus a wire crate, which I'd left in the apartment. If we did come home with a dog, I planned to hold him or her in my arms for the entire ride back to the city. We turned off the main route and followed the directions the breeder had given me over the phone. I vaguely remember the house, a raised ranch on a quiet street, but I'll never forget the welcome my husband and I got at the front door. When we rang the bell, a chorus of barks, ranging from alto to soprano, suddenly exploded. We looked through the glass panels that framed the door. In the background, we spotted a Doberman Pinscher, barking but not advancing. In the foreground were two little black dogs, yapping loudly, lunging towards the door, letting the folks who lived there know that somebody had arrived.

Pat Nigey, the woman who had run the ad, was not a member of the Schipperke Club of America. She, along with a small group of upstate New York Schipperke fanciers, who interbred their bitches and dogs, produced a few litters here and there, then sold the puppies. This time, she had one pup left, a three month old male. It was, as the cliché goes, love at first sight. This tiny little fur ball, along with his mother, Gidget, had charged the front door, while the Doberman had cautiously stayed in the background. For me, this was Dobie redux—a big dog in a small body. I was thrilled. My husband and I both handled the pup and played with Gidget. We learned that the pup's littermate had been sold several weeks before, and that this little guy now was being "brought up" by his mother and the Doberman. Nevertheless, he seemed happy and well-adjusted. We decided to buy him.

"He must be shown," Mrs. Nigey said, as Bruce took out his checkbook to pay for our new buddy.

"Of course," I replied. That Westminster clip I'd seen on tv skittered through my brain. I pictured myself trotting around the ring with my handsome little Schippie, winning ribbons and getting applause. Though we hadn't set out to acquire a show dog, this was an added bonus. I could learn something new, and while I didn't see it as a long term career, "dog handler" looked like the next step in my search for something to do with myself in middle age. It was better than bike messenger.

I told Mrs. Nigey that my husband had allergic reactions to certain dogs. When we used to visit Buster and his human family, Bruce's eyes watered, his face itched and puffed up with hives, and he sneezed as loudly as a walrus. All this happened without Buster ever touching him. Mrs. Nigey understood. She said that if we wanted to, we could take the puppy on trial. If after a week, things didn't work out, we could return him and get a full refund. I smiled. I told Mrs. Nigey, that I planned to keep the puppy. She could have my husband, and she wouldn't have to pay me a dime.

Although Mercury belonged to both of us, I won the naming rights. After all, I was the person who had done all the research, and I was the one who had spotted that ad in the *Times*. I chose Mercury, to remind me of the messenger I hadn't become. In hindsight, this was a good thing. Riding a bike in New York City traffic makes white water rafting look tame. Now that I was a dog mother, with a little Schipperke to raise and protect, I dared not try anything as foolish as zigzagging around town on a bike, racing cabs, and maybe getting hit by a bus or killed like that poor 20 year old messenger, nailed by a flat bed truck back in 2006. With my new little charge, I was revved up to enjoy at least another 15 or 16 years on this earth, the typical Schipperke lifespan.

Mercury enchanted us. He looked like a furry piglet or a baby bear with the energy level of a type A executive. He'd zip around the apartment like a black balloon losing air, then grab a toy and toss it over his head. In time, I taught him to take his collar off a nail in the hall, which I'd placed at Schipperke level. I can still see him twirling around when my husband or I asked, "Do you want to go out?" Then in a more excited voice, as if announcing an Oscar winner, saying "Get your collar!" Mercury would gallop to the nail and bring the collar to one of us, dropping it on the floor in front of the caller's feet.

We took him to Shelter Island in the spring, just after we opened the house for the season. Every puppy I'd ever met always stayed close to its new owner. Maybe these pups were fearful or uncertain of their new surroundings. Mercury was different. He was a Schipperke. I'll never

24

forget letting him loose on our property that first day. I ran up towards the back of our two acre spread and he followed me. Then, suddenly, without any reason—no squirrel, no deer, no birds on the ground—he reversed direction and took off towards the road. This was off-season, and there wasn't much traffic, but yet my heart tumbled into my feet. I ran after him, trying to get his attention. Every few feet, I clapped and turned back, expecting him to follow, but he didn't. Now he was twenty feet from the road. Bruce was inside the house and had no idea what was happening. "Mercureeee," I shouted, but the little guy trotted onward. At the moment he entered the blacktop, I saw a car coming. I darted into the road. A few feet separated me from my pup and this vehicle. Mercury continued prancing down the road. I jumped in front of the car and raised my arms to make it stop. I yelled at the driver, a middle-aged man, demanding to know what in god's name he was rushing to that made him almost run over my puppy. He didn't answer, but his expression seemed to say, "Duh. What puppy?"

By now Mercury was curious about the goings on in the street. He slowed, and I ran to him and scooped him up in my arms. I went back to the driver and said, "This is my puppy and you almost killed him." It was more polite than saying, "You stupid fuck." I took Mercury into the house and told my husband what had happened. That ended the pup's off-leash privileges until we could fence the yard.

There's a saying in the breed that a loose Schipperke is a lost Schipperke and I saw firsthand how true this could be. Mercury was more interested in adventure than in listening to me. Years later, when I wrote a book on the breed, I emphasized the fact that Schipperkes will always think they know better than humans, the right course of action to follow. If they're off-lead and they see a squirrel, a person can call and call, but the Schip will go squirrel hunting, no matter if it means crossing a busy road. Even a title-holding obedience trained Schipperke can exhibit this independent streak.

We had the Invisible Fence® installed around the property. Most dog people are familiar with this system. Basically, an underground wire emits radio waves when the fence is turned on. The dog wears a receiver on a special collar, and then is trained not to go close to the perimeter. To reinforce this, warning flags placed in the ground show where the wire is buried. Gradually they are removed as training progresses and the dog learns the boundaries. To let the dog know that he shouldn't cross the line, the trainer shocks him once, waves a flag in a menacing way and says "Nooooo." This is the only aspect of the invisible fence program that I found upsetting. But Mercury learned quickly. I never heard him yelp again because he never crossed the line.

A couple we knew on the island, Rod and Robin, had shown and bred dogs before, and now had a Border Terrier named Ruby. Mercury loved to romp with her. He may have had other ideas as well, since we hadn't had him neutered. Though I wasn't that savvy about showing, I did know that dogs in conformation classes cannot be altered, since the purpose of these shows is to present potential breeding stock. One day Robin asked me if I'd ever gone to a match. She explained these were informal, friendly dog shows where newcomers and their dogs could get some experience. Dogs couldn't earn points towards a championship, but they could learn how to behave in the ring, how to move, and how to stand for examination by the judge. Dog owners could learn about handling. Sanctioned matches, as opposed to fun matches, were operated under guidelines set up by the American Kennel Club. She told me there was an AKC sanctioned match coming up the next month and thought there was still time to enter.

I called the Riverhead Kennel Club, the group running the match and signed up. I knew nothing about dog shows then, and when I saw that the event began at 9:00 a.m., I made sure Mercury and I arrived well in advance. We pulled into the driveway about 8:15, along with the volunteers who were helping set up. Participants began to trickle in much later. I hadn't brought Mercury's crate, so he and I walked around a bit, then sat down in the grass to wait. Our class didn't show until 11:00. Mercury was eight months old by then and still, at least to me, the cutest puppy at the match. He pranced like a little pony as I walked him around the ring. The judges fawned over him. They hadn't seen a Schipperke in a long time. One of the judges said, "I think you've got something there." I guess he saw Mercury's potential as a show dog. He suggested that I enter Riverhead's annual dog show which took place later that summer. I was elated. My little puppy was on his way to dog show stardom. I took the entry form home with me and filled it out.

I bought a show lead, a thin piece of braided nylon that had a loop at one end to go over the dog's head, forming a slip collar. I didn't know at the time that Schipperke people preferred Resco leads. Made of a leather-like material called "cordo-hyde," they scrunched easily in one's hand for a solid grip and provided better control. For a collar, they liked a gold toned "snake" chain. It created a handsome accent against the dark fur of the dog's ruff and didn't get stuck in the hair. Later, after I learned this, I bought the right accessories. I certainly didn't want to be at a disadvantage when it came to style.

Though it was over fifteen years ago, I remember some aspects of that Riverhead show very clearly. I remember going into the ring with Mercury and taking him around. I don't recall the exact number of

Schipperkes competing that day. It might've three or four. I remember stacking him on the table so the judge could examine him. We hadn't practiced this enough, I suppose, because when the judge tried to feel Mercury's testicles, to make sure both had descended, the dog shied away. We didn't win a ribbon or any points towards a championship that day, but at least I didn't stumble or fall down, like some unfortunate handlers I'd see at future shows. That's why I was stunned when the judge approached me. I remember his thin lips and his cold eyes, glaring at me from behind his rimless glasses. He said, "You should take some handling classes. How dare you come to a point show with such little experience?" I wanted to tell him that the friendly people at the Riverhead match had urged me to enter, but he had already turned away.

Chapter 5

Back Stage Mama

That fall, back in the city, I found a dog school offering show handling classes. In was located in a run-down building on 23rd Street just off Eighth Avenue. I had a friend, Anna, who was a dog walker in my neighborhood. She wanted to learn how to show her Doberman, a dark, handsome fellow with the temperament of a saint. Together we signed up for the beginner's class. Anna had a car which made it easy for us to get downtown. She'd pick me up at my apartment on the corner of Fifth Avenue and 101st Street around 6:30 for the 7 p.m. class. It was a straight run down the avenue, and usually traffic was light. We didn't worry about parking, because in those days, there were plenty of spaces on the street in Chelsea. It hadn't yet become gentrified. One night Anna's car suddenly stopped dead near the Frick Museum at 70th Street. She managed to coast to the curb and guide it into a "no parking" spot. She planned to call AAA and have it towed to her mechanic later on, but our immediate goal was to get to the dog school. Every cab we hailed slowed, saw the Doberman, and sped away. I told Anna to hide the dog behind her skirt. She was a large woman so this was easy to do. I held Mercury in my arms. The few cabs that stopped to pick us up floored it the moment Anna's dog stepped out from behind her clothing. Finally, a taxi pulled up. I told the driver we'd pay extra if he took us. In the cab, the Doberman lay down and slept while Mercury kept a keen eye on the man behind the wheel.

Our class was an interesting mix of dog show hopefuls. There was an Afghan, a Maltese, the Doberman, a Viszla, a Bulldog, a Westie and my Schipperke. There were no mixed breeds since our dogs were all candidates for American Kennel Club championships and therefore had to represent one of AKC's recognized breeds. I had mailed Mercury's registration papers right after we'd bought him. Mrs. Nigey had said that I didn't have to use her kennel name, Kebrill, but since I wasn't planning on becoming a breeder and establishing my own kennel, I let it stand. I registered him as Kebrill's Mercury. In time, as I met more people in the dog world, I learned something interesting. Most Schipperke Club members, as well as serious show kennels in other breeds, insist on a written contract and co-ownership of any dog or bitch they sell as a show prospect. This gives the breeder control over what shows will be entered, and what, if any, breedings will take place. An arrangement such as this can provide a novice with an opportunity to learn the ins and outs of showing. It can also result in nasty custody fights, just like when people divorce. I was glad Mrs. Nigey sold her dogs outright.

After the Westminster Kennel Club Dog Show was over in February, there weren't any shows in my area until March. Our handling classes were almost finished and most of us were eager to take a shot at entering a *bona fide* AKC show.

I decided to enter Mercury in a show in Pennsylvania, which was a drivable distance from the city. I planned to limit myself to places I could reach in three hours or less, except for back to back shows where I'd stay overnight. My husband had no interest in going along.

Cars of that era had no navigational systems so I had to follow a map. This was easy until I exited the Pennsylvania Turnpike. Then I turned left when I should've turned right. I remember driving and driving on a small blacktop road. Farms flanked the route, but I saw no signs for a dog show or even for the fairgrounds where it was being held. There were also no stores or people in sight. Finally, after ten minutes of driving, I spotted a small grocery store. The clerk inside told me the bad news. I had to go back the other way for about twenty miles. Luckily, I'd left plenty of extra time, and as it turned out, I needed it. Mercury and I arrived at the fairgrounds with only fifteen minutes to spare.

Mercury didn't win any points that day, but I remember the judge. She was a direct contrast to the snarly-faced fellow who had criticized me at Riverhead. It must've been clear to her that I was a novice, and that Mercury hadn't been to many shows. But she liked him. After the class, she told me he was a nice dog, but that I should put a little weight on him and let him grow up. This brought to mind a tune that was popular in the 1950s, "Little Things Mean a Lot." Her remarks that day gave me a needed boost.

I entered a few more shows with the same results, no points towards our championship. At one of them, I ran into two young women I'd met at Riverhead. Carolyn was showing her Schipperke, Tuxedo, as a Special, which meant he'd already completed his championship and was vying for Best of Breed, and Krista had a bitch of her own breeding in the classes. It was clear I still had a lot to learn, but one of the things I picked up pretty quickly is that familiar faces count. Judges get used to seeing certain handlers in show after show. They are more likely to pay attention to a dog at the end of such a person's lead. Carolyn and Krista were these kinds of faces. Carolyn said, for a fee, she or Krista could finish Mercury. In dog show lingo, this meant earning him the fifteen points needed to be certified a champion. I hired them.

At the very next show, on a Saturday, Mercury came home with his first point. The day after that, he won another. Clearly Carolyn and Krista were worth the money. I liked that they were photogenic, too, especially Krista. She was tall and blonde, very Scandinavian looking, although I had no idea of her background. In any event, I always made sure they had official dog show pictures taken whenever Mercury won. These girls were young, in their early twenties, I'd guessed, but to their credit, they always knew what clothes to wear in order to show off the dog.

Mercury needed majors, an award of three to five points, depending on the number of entries in his breed. This was tricky in Schipperkes. There weren't that many competing in our area, which meant there were few shows where a major could be won. A dog or bitch needed to win six major points under two different judges as part of its championship package, the rest could be single points. I knew of a fellow whose Schipperke had accumulated 32 single points, but never won any majors and therefore never became a champion. Maybe he should've hired Carolyn or Krista.

The search for majors brought me to a three day cluster of dog shows upstate New York one weekend in August. This was outside my three hour drive limit so I found a "dog motel" for Mercury and me. I probably should explain that label since, to many people, it may sound like a boarding kennel. But no, it's my description of hotels and motels that have seen better days, those bypassed by tourists and conventioneers, and often located in the not-so-prime parts of a city or town. What better way to fill those empty rooms than to rent them to show people and their canine companions?

That weekend, Carolyn and Krista had entered out-of-state shows with their own Schipperkes and were not available to handle Mercury. I decided to show him myself. By now I'd bought a Resco lead and gold snake chain, so Mercury looked ever so fine. I can't remember what I wore, but in the absence of Krista and Carolyn, I'd bought a few outfits that said "dog handler" without saying "Saks Fifth Avenue." In other words, I found some mainstream fashions that formed a contrasting background for my little black dog and were loose enough in their cut to allow me to move around the ring without impediment. On my feet, I sported flat shoes with non-slip soles. This was not the arena for Manolo Blahnik or Jimmy Choo.

The steward called our class and we entered the ring in catalog order, which is the way things usually unfolded. I caught Merc's attention with bait, some gross tasting liver I'd cooked myself according to a recipe my Doberman friend, Anna, had given me. I thought I did a good job with Mercury. But to my dismay, we came in third, which was actually last, since there were only two other competitors. A woman standing ringside with a Schipperke that had beaten us, took me aside and said I ought to put a handler on my dog. She introduced me to Jerry, the fellow standing alongside her, and I hired him for the next day's show. What a difference a face makes, and of course, expertise. Mercury picked up his first major with Jerry, a juicy three points. One month later, at another show with Carolyn, he won a four point major. Mercury was two points shy of the fifteen needed to be crowned "champion," but the very next day, again with Carolyn, he got them. I was thrilled when she told me. Champion Kebrill's Mercury, now that had an impressive ring.

Dogs (and bitches) become "champions of record," until all their awards can be verified by the AKC. Sometimes this takes a month or two. But I couldn't wait to show off my new champion. I entered him in Brookhaven Kennel Club to compete in Best of Breed. This is a class for champions, although the dog or bitch that won the points from the other classes—Open, Bred by Exhibitor, American Bred, and the various puppy classes to name a few—are entitled to compete against the "big guys." That day, there were no other Schipperkes at the show, so Mercury was a shoo-in. The photo of him and me, and Mr. Bernfeld, the judge, sits on the mantle at my country house. Later in this book, it will be obvious why I identified this judge by name.

I believe in Newton's Third Law, that for every action there is a reaction. By extension, I believe that every happy moment in a person's life is counterbalanced by heartache. Shortly after Brookhaven, I sent in my Westminster entry. Back then, entries had to be mailed and postmarked no earlier than 12:01 a.m. on the day entries opened. I pictured some gnome at the dog show's offices, magnifying glass in hand, scrutinizing those postmarks, then perhaps gleefully tossing out the ones that didn't comply. I smiled to myself as I imagined that this would have been the perfect off-season job for that creepy judge from the Riverhead Kennel Club Dog show.

Although New York is known as the city that never sleeps, I suspected this didn't apply to the Post Office. No harm in waiting until daylight, I reasoned. Back then, getting into Westminster wasn't the competitive frenzy that it is today. Shortly before 8 a.m., I took a bus to the main post office. I wanted to be first on line when it opened. A few people were ahead of me, probably folks late with their rent payments or Con Ed bills. A few minutes later, it was my turn. I asked that my entry be hand cancelled to insure the early post mark. I'd heard from other dog people that this was the key to acceptance. I couldn't believe it. Mercury and I were going to Madison Square Garden. The non-sporting breeds, which include Schipperkes, were scheduled for Monday, February 14th, Valentine's Day. But it was also the eve of my fiftieth birthday, and, as a gift to myself, I intended to show him. This time I wouldn't use a handler. What better way to enter the next half-century of my life than to be part of the Westminster Kennel Club Dog Show, the "Oscars" of the canine world?

In November, I received a letter from a woman at the AKC's Event Records Department. As I read it, I felt as though someone had punched me hard in the stomach. Apparently Mercury wasn't a champion. I studied the attachment which detailed the shows he'd been in, and how many points he'd earned in each. Towards the end of the list, there it was: Westchester Kennel Club. One point. Carolyn had told me he'd earned two. How could she have made such a dreadful mistake?

Carolyn had thought, wrongly, that two points had been at stake at that Westchester show. When I phoned her, her attitude shocked me. Instead of a big apology and an offer to send back the tip I'd given her for finishing him, or perhaps donate it to an animal charity, she told me he'd just have to go out again.

"Not with you," I said. As soon as I hung up, I called Jerry and told him what had happened. He said he could handle Mercury for me at an upstate show in December, but I had to hurry. The deadline for entries was approaching. Mercury became a champion at that show, finishing with one point to spare. I was so proud of him. Even my husband was thrilled. Though he never had come to any of the other dog shows, he announced he would go to the Garden.

Unlike most show dogs who live in kennels or in households with multiple dogs, Mercury was our "only child." We often took him with us when we ate out at sidewalk cafes. People stopped and admired him, always asking what kind of dog he was, then allowing that they'd never heard of Schipperkes. We took him to Puerto Rico in his Sherpa® bag, sneaking him onto the plane as carry-on baggage. In the pre-9/11 era, we had no qualms doing that. Charging for a pet in the cabin while allowing all sorts of non-animal carry-ons for free, made us rebellious. Besides, no one ever asked for his ticket. Like most Schipperkes, Mercury was an excellent traveler. He never barked or whined, and thankfully, never passed gas.

I used to call him "my little fox," because that's what he resembled, a fox without a tail. He'd sit in the bathroom doorway when I was getting ready to go out and stare at me. I am convinced animals experience emotions. Some smile. Some pout when they don't get their way. In Mercury's eyes I saw jealousy. It was as clear as if he could say, "I'll take you to that black tie dinner. Leave your husband at home in a crate." Yet he never indulged in destructive behavior, except once, when he was a puppy. We were spending the weekend at our country place. Bruce had left his socks and underwear on the floor after getting undressed for bed. The next day, I noticed something red in Mercury's stool. I was ready to rush him to the vet, when my husband came downstairs, holding a pair of red cotton briefs with a hole in them. "Look what this bad dog did," he said. But he was laughing.

I taught Mercury some tricks. Like a retriever, he'd jump in the bay and fetch a stick. He was a natural swimmer. He could twirl around and dance on his hind legs, shake hands and fall down when "shot." This amused the police officers who used to hang out at the entrance to Central Park, near our apartment building, looking for drug dealers. "Dead dog," I'd say, forming my hand into a gun. On cue, Mercury lay down. The cops loved him.

Mercury became a champion in time for Christmas and we rewarded him with extra toys. He loved to unwrap them himself, ripping the paper with his rat-catcher's teeth. I had already received my crate pass and judging program for Westminster, yet it was still hard for me to believe that in less than two months, we were going to the Garden. Every day I practiced gaiting Mercury and stacking him. I had my friend, Anna, play judge and go over him, checking his "b and b's," his bite and his balls. Mercury seemed ready. I was the one who still needed work.

Chapter 6

Winter Chill

In January, I traveled to Florida to visit my parents for Ukrainian Christmas. I left on a Thursday, planning to return on Monday. My husband didn't want to take care of Mercury. He said he might have to go out of town on business, though he wasn't sure. I've never kenneled any of my dogs, then or now, and his reluctance to watch our "kid" disappointed me. Anna could've walked the dog during the day. All he'd have to do was feed him and walk him in the morning and at night. But the decision was made. Mercury was headed to my brother-in-law Don's in New Jersey. Don had a Bull Mastiff named Maggie, and she and Mercury played together whenever Don and his family visited us on Shelter Island. We always took Mercury with us when we visited them, and since they also had the Invisible Fence®, I'd trained Mercury to respect the boundaries. That morning, when I put Mercury into his crate in the car for the trip to New Jersey, a strange sadness came over me. Like a puff of wind, it was fleeting, then gone. "You be a good boy," I remember saying to him.

My flight to Fort Myers took off just before the control tower grounded every other plane. Snow had started falling at noon, and it was piling up fast. By one o'clock, the de-icers were stressed. The captain announced that we might have to deplane. Good, I thought. I really didn't want to take off in that mess. But shortly after his announcement, we taxied onto the runway and flew into the gray-white swirl. We passed out of the storm, into the sun and the rest of the trip went smoothly.

The next day, January 7th, was Ukrainian Christmas. My mom had cooked a ham and my dad had bought a batch of stone crab claws, not an ethnic specialty, but something he knew I liked. We drank Champagne, and Dad put on polka records. He and my mom were dancing around the living room when the telephone rang. It was Bruce. He said Mercury had been hit by a car. Don had let the dogs out into the yard, but only Maggie came back. The snow had turned to sleet by then, creating an extra slippery surface. Perhaps Mercury, with his short show dog nails, had slid over the Invisible Fence® barrier. Or perhaps the radio waves hadn't penetrated the huge amount of snow and ice that had accumulated on the ground, on top of a previous snow storm, preventing him from hearing the warning beeps. We will never know. In a panic, Don and his wife, Lynda, grabbed flashlights and searched for the dog. They found him down the street, lying in a snow bank by the side of the road. They rushed him to their vet in the next town. He took x-rays and diagnosed a serious spinal cord injury. He suggested the dog be put down.

Bruce had already returned to the city when Don and Lynda called him. Because of the blizzard conditions, he couldn't go back to New Jersey. He also couldn't bring himself to have Mercury euthanized. He called the vet and said he would pick up Mercury on Saturday and take him to the Animal Medical Center in Manhattan. If there was any hope of saving Mercury, this facility, with its state-of-the-art equipment and expert staff of veterinary specialists, was it. But bad luck wouldn't leave us alone. I couldn't get a flight home until 7 a.m. on Sunday, and because most runways in New York were still iced in, it was delayed several hours. By then, Mercury had been lying in a crate at the Medical Center, dosed with painkillers since Saturday afternoon. I'll never forget walking into the ward. Crates of injured animals stood side by side in a corridor whose lights had been dimmed to create a peaceful setting. When Mercury saw me, he cried. So did I. I could tell from the puffiness of my husband's eyes that he'd spent the last two days crying as well.

Additional x-rays taken the day before showed a single back fracture of the vertebra L1. The broken piece had lodged in Mercury's spinal cord. The doctors on duty said they could try surgery, though they gave him very slim chances of recovery—less than five percent. In addition, the orthopedic surgeon who could perform such a demanding operation was out of town until Monday. Though we knew too much time had elapsed for a good outcome to such a devastating injury, we decided to go ahead.

On the morning of January 10th, Mercury had surgery. I sat by the phone waiting for a call from the Animal Medical Center. Instead, I received a call from the show secretary at MB-F, the organization that handles the entries for the Westminster Kennel Club Dog Show. It was more bad news. Because Mercury hadn't finished his championship until December, past the deadline for *bona fide* entries, he was ineligible to attend Westminster. I explained what had happened to him, and that he couldn't possibly compete in the show. The MB-F caller then informed me his name would not appear in the catalog. My voice quavered as I asked if they could please make an exception. It was, after all, Carolyn's fault that he hadn't finished by the deadline. But they said no. By the time the veterinarian called, I was expecting more bad news. While his call wasn't filled with optimism, it did give me some hope. He told me Mercury was resting and that we'd have to take it day by day to see how or if he'd recuperate.

Five days later, we took Mercury home. To hold his spine in place and align the vertebrae, the surgeon had inserted a rectangular frame beneath the shaved off coat on his back. It looked as though a shoe box had been sewn under his skin. My little fox was a sorry sight. He couldn't bark because of all the tubes that had been placed in his throat during the surgery. He could only make thin, croaking noises, each one an echo of my breaking heart. Mercury's hind end was paralyzed. He had no sensation in his legs and no ability to control elimination. Stools emerged when ready, but urination required help. The veterinarian showed me how to apply pressure to his bladder with my fingertips. For the next few weeks, I slept on the floor, next to his bed and cared for him.

One of my horse friends told me of a veterinarian upstate who practiced alternative medicine. He was well-respected at her barn where, through acupuncture treatments, many a lame horse had been cured. We decided to have him take a look at Mercury. Six weeks had passed since the surgery. Mercury was getting stronger, though he still could only lie on his side on his cushion. We carried him into the car and put him in his crate. The veterinarian studied the x-rays we'd brought with us. He squeezed Mercury's pads, hoping for a reaction, but there was none. He thought acupuncture might help. There was a slim chance it would stimulate the dog's deadened nerves, but it was a very slim chance.

For the next two weeks, Mercury received bi-weekly treatments upstate. Then we found a practitioner closer to home in the city. We bought a wire crate big enough for a Great Dane and put it in the bedroom so Mercury could sleep there. He had begun to pull himself off his cushion during the night, and we were afraid he'd bang into furniture and damage the frame on his back. We bought a used stroller in a thrift shop and took him out every morning for a stroll in Central Park. People stopped to look, surprised to see a dog in the carriage instead of a baby.

One afternoon, while Mercury was lying on his cushion on the sofa, his hind legs suddenly kicked out. I stared at him. Was this the miracle I was hoping for? Immediately, I called the vet. But he said it was a reflex action that had no link to the nerve cells. I massaged Mercury's pads as if I could brush away the veterinarian's words. But the feet felt cold and lifeless.

In April, on the veterinarian's recommendation, we cut back the acupuncture to once a week. By the end of that month, it became clear the treatments weren't working. There was nothing more that alternative medicine could do to help us. The orthopedic surgeon from the Animal Medical Center examined Mercury again and took more x-rays. He concluded that the dog would never regain use of his hind end. My husband and I looked at each other with tears in our eyes. But we never embraced or hugged. We were like strangers at a funeral, grieving but not connected.

I bought a neoprene sling that supported Mercury's rear and took him on short walks in the park. Sometimes, I removed the harness and placed him in the grass. His shoulders and forelegs were strong enough so he could pull himself forward, dragging his hind end. It was an inspiring yet sad sight to see this animal trying so hard to be the dog he had been before.

Mercury loved to have his belly scratched. One day, while I was tickling him, I saw something run across his stomach. The dark critter stood out against his white skin. I knew it was a flea. I grabbed the special comb, ran it through his fur, caught the pest, and flushed it down the toilet. With all the surgery Mercury had had, the baths and the antiseptics, it was outrageous that a flea or fleas still were feasting on him. Three years had passed since Hurricane Bob hit Eastern Long Island in August, 1991. That was the month and year I discovered fleas. Up until then, I'd never seen one, except in veterinary pamphlets and books.

The morning Bob was due, I was at our Shelter Island house with Mercury. I remember how gray it was that day, and how still. Bruce had taken the early bus back to the city to go to work. Despite the hurricane forecasts, I decided to stay put with Mercury. Soon the wind picked up. Though our house had survived the hurricane of 1938, only losing its chimney, I wasn't sure how it would stand up to Bob. We had glassed in the porch when we did some renovations shortly after we'd bought the place. By mid-morning, the storm hit. Then the power went out. I sat on the steps leading to the porch and watched Bob toss branches around like Frisbees®. I hoped he wouldn't send any towards the house. Mercury was sitting next to me. I ran my fingers through his coat,

37

scratching him to reassure him. That's when I felt the grains. I thought perhaps he'd gotten into some plants with seeds or briars.

The hurricane doused the island with rain, and the strong winds uprooted trees and ripped boats from their anchors. No one had been ready for a storm of such strength, but Mercury and I survived it just fine. Late in the afternoon, when Bob had passed and the sun came out, I put Mercury in the car and drove back to the city. The next day, I called our regular veterinarian and described these "seeds." He gave me the bad news: my dog had fleas. The "seeds" were flea excrement. For the next few years, we battled these pests. Baths, dips, Frontline®, daily rakings with the flea comb, no matter what we tried, Mercury always had a resident flea or two. They particularly liked to hide in the area around his scrotum. As a show dog, and a potential stud, he was not neutered, and his testicles provided these pests with their preferred warm, moist environment. I spent a lot of time flea hunting. To make it easier for me to comb through his underbelly, I had trained him to lie down on his back when I asked, "Who has fleas?" He already knew "dead dog," so for this, he only had to roll over a bit further.

But now, as an invalid, he couldn't do any of his tricks, nor could he roll over to help me get a stab at those fleas. Our veterinarian, whom we'd kept informed about the specialists' diagnoses, suggested that we consider getting a wheeled cart which attached to the dog's hindquarters. I'd seen a few old dogs in the park with these devices, and I suppose, for some owners, this was a way to keep their cherished companions around a bit longer. But I couldn't see this for Mercury. He wasn't even four years old, and with no hope for recovery, it seemed cruel to sentence him to years in the canine equivalent of a wheelchair. Yet his spirit was keen, he was eating his food, and his front end grew stronger by the day. In fact, he'd learned how to prop himself up to the extent that he sometimes fooled us into thinking he was standing on all fours. How, in good conscience, could we euthanize him now?

In mid-May, Mercury developed a hot spot on his back. It rose from his body like an angry boil, and had erupted in a place dangerously close to his spine. He had never had one before, and I had never seen one, though I had heard about them from other friends who had dogs. I checked my veterinary manual, a bible I relied on for everything from doggy dental problems to mammary tumors and more. This was years before the Internet became the comprehensive and readily accessible information source it is today. I learned that hot spots, or acute moist pyoderma are skin infections that suddenly appear, and are oozing, nasty sores. I looked at my dog. That certainly described the ugly thing that had sprouted on him. Hot spots happen because something irritates the dog's skin, such as flea bites or allergies. I immediately thought back to that pest I had captured and flushed down the toilet. It seems it had left some cohorts behind. Poor Mercury. I didn't know if he was able to feel any sensation at the site of the hot spot. The manual said most dogs will try to scratch or lick at the sore, but of course, he could do neither. I had a small bottle of tea tree oil in my medicine cabinet. I used it on myself to cure everything from mosquito bites to athlete's foot, so I figured it might work on the hot spot. I applied some, and within a few hours, the hot spot collapsed. The next day, I called the Animal Medical Center and left a message for the veterinarian who had treated Mercury. A short time later, the receptionist called back and said to bring him in. I hopped in a cab with Mercury on my lap. He could walk with the neoprene sling, but I carried him. I needed to hold him, and I think he needed to be held. By nature, I am not a pessimistic person, but during that taxi ride that morning, I sensed it was the beginning of the end.

The veterinarian who examined Mercury prescribed the antibiotic Clavamox. This is commonly given in cases of infection, and the doctor was concerned that some internal infection might have developed at the site of the hot spot. I've long forgotten the dosage or how many times a day I had to give him his pill, but I do remember the results. Mercury got diarrhea from the Clavamox.

At first, I administered the usual treatment. I withheld water and food for 24 hours. Then I cooked up a batch of boiled rice and fed that to him. It ran out of his body like water. I added small pieces of boiled chicken breasts. I gave him a dose of Kaopectate. Nothing stayed inside. I called the vet again. He said to continue with what I was doing. Then I called Pat Nigey. I asked her what she thought I should do. She said, "He will tell you when it's time." Even today, her words make me tear up. She knew her dogs, and I still can see Mercury, lying on my sofa in the apartment, his keen, bright eyes, having turned dull, his prick ears, lying flat against his head, his expression saying, "Please, Ma, help me."

The veterinarian with whom I spoke at the Medical Center had said to continue withholding food and water, but Pat Nigey's words nagged at my brain. I looked at my precious Mercury, and I knew it was over. I called Bruce and told him that I would contact the veterinarian on Shelter Island. We had agreed, way before, that when the time came, we would take Mercury to our house and bury him in our yard.

So many things in life seem connected, if only people took the time to step back and notice them. I had always felt this way about Jackie Kennedy Onassis. I used to see her everywhere in the city—at the ballet, in restaurants, in Central Park, cross-country skiing with Caroline. I saw her in a limousine, speeding east on 86th street, a slim cigar or cigarillo sticking out of her mouth, her huge dark glasses hiding half her face, but fooling no one. I used to joke with my friends that she was following *me*. So, when Jackie died on May 19th, 1994, I felt a sense of loss. I had never met her, of course, but I felt a connection, and this carried over to Mercury. I have an old magazine photo of Jackie as a young woman, standing in front of what would now be a vintage automobile. It made my skin prickle when I noticed the hubcaps. They read: "Mercury."

Two days after Jackie died, we put Mercury down. I had called the veterinarian on Shelter Island and explained the situation. I'd given him the phone number of the doctor at the Animal Medical Center in case he wanted to verify that the dog had indeed gone through everything we said he had endured. I remember driving out to the island that day. It was one of those beautiful spring days when the shrubbery flanking the Long Island Expressway provided a border of soft pinks and whites. It was just Mercury and me in the car, the way it had been when we traveled to dog shows. I'd hoped my husband might've come with us on this last ride, but he was working and had decided to take the bus later that evening. Half way through our trip, Mercury had a nasty bout of diarrhea. It stunk, as we used to say when we were kids, "to high heaven." I stopped the car and picked him up, out of the mess. He looked forlorn, ashamed, embarrassed. I told him everything was all right, though we both knew that it wasn't.

I had also contacted a carpenter on the island who had been the contractor on the renovations to our house. He knew Mercury from the times he had stopped by to get paid, and he always enjoyed petting him. When I asked if he would make a coffin, he was stunned and saddened. I told him I needed it by mid-day on Saturday.

That Saturday morning, just after sunrise, I took Mercury to the beach one last time. He wore his harness and managed to drag himself along though the sand with my help. I watched him point his nose to the wind and sniff the sea. I wondered if he knew he'd never come here again. We had an appointment with the vet at 11. Every minute until then seemed an eternity. My husband was crying and I was crying. I have never known time to pass so slowly or with so much agony. Waiting. Our life for the past few months had consisted of waiting. Waiting in vets' offices for examinations and hopefully, cures, and now waiting once again for a veterinarian to deal the *coup de grace*.

The Shelter Island veterinarian specialized in farm animals, but as more and more people came from the city as vacation homeowners, they brought their pets, and he branched out into dogs and cats. Yet he was a big animal doc at heart. I remember one day when my friend's pony had a bad attack of colic. There was no hope for the little Shetland, so my friend called the Doc. He arrived within minutes. He told her to usher her children into the house. A few minutes later a shot rang out. Pony had been "euthanized." So, it was with some reluctance that we brought Mercury to him. He greeted us at the door to his clinic, which was next to the garage, attached to the side of his house.

"How are you folks, today?" he asked.

I swallowed my tears and said, "We've been better." I was holding Mercury. Bruce stood behind me, sniveling. He had been a wreck all morning. The fact that this was good-by to our dear Mercury hit him hard, and he was unable to do anything except drive to the vet's while I held our dog in my lap. In the examination room, the vet gave Mercury valium to relax him before the final injection. The vet's hands were huge, the kind we used to refer to as "hamhocks" back in less politically correct days. I marveled that he could be so delicate with my poor, dying dog. I held Mercury as he injected the heart-stopping drug. In a minute or so, he felt the dog's neck and body, searching, for a heartbeat or any sign of life. There were none. He nodded to me. I couldn't fight back the tears. At the reception desk, my husband paid the fee. He'd run out of tissues and his nose was dripping, but he didn't seem to care.

The veterinarian left us with one important tip. "Folks," he said, "when you bury the dog, don't put him in a plastic bag. No sir. Because this is what happens. There's gases released when the body decays, so if it's wrapped in plastic, it's gonna explode. Yup. I know of cases where folks have put a pet in the ground, only to have it come blasting out of the earth. So, you folks be careful."

I stared at my husband. He stared at me. The vet offered his hand for a shake. I can't recall whether either of us took it. We walked out to the car. I had Mercury wrapped in a hospital pad. The vet had said, as the muscles relaxed in death, there could be some unexpected elimination. But Mercury was as clean in death as he'd been in life, and nothing came out. Mercury was "my little fox," but he was also "the Prince of Dogs," superbly elegant and regal. When he became champion, I'd had a tee shirt made up with his photo and the line, Mercury, Prince of Dogs. I still have it. By now, it must've been washed over a hundred times, yet the picture and tag line remain, not as clear as when they were new, but in a better condition that I ever would have imagined. I still wear this shirt, and when I do, I think of him and the short, but precious time we spent together.

We returned home in silence. Our carpenter friend hadn't shown up with the coffin. I wondered if he'd been too overcome with grief to complete it. I decided to drive to his house, about three minutes down the road. I half-expected to see him sobbing on his saw horse. But when I pulled into the driveway, he wasn't crying. He was chatting with someone, who, as it turned out, was another customer. I interrupted and asked about the coffin. He said he'd have it done within the hour. Coffins or renovations, it didn't make much difference. Workmen never delivered their jobs on time.

The previous winter I'd met a friend for lunch downtown, in Soho. After we ate, we decided to walk off some calories and go window shopping. A few blocks from the restaurant, in front of the French Connection, we saw the sign: Sale. We were drawn inside, as if a giant magnet were aimed at us, rendering us helpless in the face of money-saving shopping possibilities. On a table with marked down, hand-made sweaters, one caught my eye. It was a fanciful cardigan, in hot pink and navy blue with knitted yellow stars cascading down the front and the back. Interwoven, or should I say, inter-knitted, was this phrase: The Winter the Stars Fell. My friend bought one, and I bought the other, wiping out the entire sale stock of that particular design in size small. On the morning of Mercury's death, I retrieved that sweater from the cedar chest in the bedroom where I had put it away for the summer. I brought it downstairs and waited for the carpenter.

He finally arrived a half hour later. He was a burly man and, perhaps out of guilt for his tardiness, volunteered to dig the grave. The coffin he'd made was shaped like a box to accommodate Mercury's square cushion. I had given him dimensions beforehand, by phone. After we came home from the vet, I had taken Mercury out of the car and lay him on his side on the cushion. It was covered in red plaid fabric, and he, a black dog, had always looked strikingly handsome against that bold background. Bruce came out of the house and helped me place the cushion into the coffin. I picked up the sweater and draped it over Mercury. *The winter the stars fell.* Rest in peace, my friend.

Chapter 7

Monkey

We buried Mercury under the willow tree, at the point where our property slants gently uphill towards the woods. It was a spot I could see from the kitchen window, and by next spring, I planned to have flowers growing there, provided the deer didn't eat them. The carpenter had finished his job, shoveling the dirt into the hole and tamping it down with a spade. He expressed his sympathy, and headed towards his van, which he'd parked in our driveway. As he walked past me, I noticed his eyes were watery. Bruce and I went back into the house. I had a headache from all the crying I'd done over the last few days. He went upstairs to nap. I don't remember how the rest of the day passed. Did we have dinner? Did we drink wine? I just don't know. I do recall placing some flowers from the garden on the fresh mound near the willow. They might have been daffodils or forsythia. I've forgotten what was blooming at that time in May. Somehow I slept through the night, and Bruce slept as well. It was the sleep of exhaustion, of a weariness so intense that thunder could've exploded over our roof and we never would have heard it.

The next morning, I went downstairs to the kitchen. Bruce was pouring his coffee. The house was silent. There was no little black dog prancing around, looking for breakfast. There was no invalid on a cushion, waiting to be fed and petted. Mercury had been a presence, a source of energy and life. Even when injured, he had fulfilled his role as man's and woman's best friend. My husband and I looked at each other, and again, we cried.

43

We returned to the city. I continued to take my morning walks in the park, avoiding people who knew me. I couldn't bear to talk about Mercury. Later in the week, I called Pat Nigey. I tried to keep from choking up when I spoke, but I know Pat could hear the tears in my voice. I could hear them in hers, as well. Then Pat told me the news. She'd bred Gidget one last time. She had planned to retire her, but when Mercury got injured, Pat suspected he wasn't going to make it. She thought maybe I'd want another Schipperke.

People react to losing a pet in different ways. One of my friends confided she'd never get another dog. The emotional pain of putting down her 15 year-old Beagle was too fierce. Another changed breeds. And yet another waited years before she could bring herself to get another dog. Mercury's death was as painful to me as the loss of Rusty. Yet I couldn't stand the emptiness he'd left behind. Sharing one's life with a dog, a cat, a bird or even a hamster or mouse means knowing that sadness and heartbreak await down the road. But I was ready to face that. I'd become addicted to Schipperkes. I needed to see those dark, curious eyes looking at me the moment I woke up in the morning. I needed to see that special doggy smile, showing a flash of white teeth against shiny, black fur. And I needed to laugh at silly antics such as grabbing a toy and shaking it "to death" as if it were a live rat. Bruce felt the same way.

Gidget's litter had been born on Mother's Day, which fell on May 8th that year. She had two males and one female. Two to four puppies are normal for the breed. Pat said I could come up to see them when they were a month old. Normally, breeders don't allow visitors until the puppies are ready to be sold, at eight to twelve weeks, for fear that people might carry in germs or viruses. But Pat knew I was hurting, and I accepted her invitation. I had already decided that whatever pup we took, whether it was male or female, its call name was going to be Monkey. Yes, I intended to get another show dog, and the call name is just that—the familiar, everyday name for the dog, like Twinkie, as opposed to the name that goes on the registration papers: Twinkletown's Two Timin' Tootsie.

For me, "monkey" embodied the Schipperke personality, clever and intelligent, yet spirited and quirky. I couldn't wait to see the pups. People often say they resemble baby bears, and they do, in miniature. While a bear cub, at birth, can weigh up to a pound, a Schipperke puppy is a tiny three ounces. These pups, though, had a full month of life under their little bellies, so they had developed past the three ounce mark. Furry, fuzzy, precious little critters, their barks were high pitched squeaks, as they tumbled over one another, nipping and playing. I sat on the sofa and watched them. Pat pointed to one of the males and said he was the one she had chosen for us. Even at this early stage of his life, she thought he'd make the best show dog. As Pat had instructed, I had washed my hands and taken off my shoes. I got down on the floor and let the pups sniff my fingers.

The next four weeks passed slowly. I can't remember how I filled my days, but somehow they crept by, one after another, hour after hour. I tried not to think about Mercury, but his presence was everywhere, in the kitchen drawer where I'd tucked his collars, on the hook in the closet where his show lead still hung, and in a heartwarming photograph of him and my husband, smoking "cigars." I'd taken that picture the previous winter, on a snowy day at our Shelter Island house. Bruce, cigar in mouth, and dressed like a farmer in overalls and a cap, was kneeling, holding Mercury on his knee. Mercury was "smoking" a pine cone.

Finally, as July approached, excitement about our new puppy pushed mourning into the background. I had bought a new collar and lead, plus a few new toys. Though Mercury's gear was perfectly usable, I wanted our new "kid" to start off with new things. In mid-July, we drove up to Pat's. The three puppies were out in the yard. One of them stood under a shrub, reluctant to come greet us. This was most un-Schipperke like, and I asked Pat if that was the male she'd selected for us. She said, no, it was the other male, but that we should take our time and play with all the pups. One of them kept coming to us, smelling us, and letting us pet it. I picked up the puppy and ran my fingers through its soft, downy fur.

"See how he loves us already," I said to Pat.

She smiled. "Turn "him" over," she said.

It was the little female. We went inside, and the puppies started playing with a small toy. One of them shoved the others out of the way and grabbed it. The toyless ones stood aside and cried. Bruce said, "That's the one for us. Look how outgoing he is."

Pat smiled again. "It's the little girl," she said.

During the course of the hour we spent at Pat's, the female pup kept coming over to us, sniffing, pushing her brothers around, and enchanting us. All the pups were adorable, but the girl sizzled with personality and spirit. These were desirable qualities for a show dog. We decided to buy her. Since she was born on Mother's Day, I registered her as "Kebrill's Mothersday Miracle." I already was picturing her at the end of Mercury's show lead, trotting around the ring with me at the Garden, a champion, just like he was. Of course, her call name was Monkey.

We paid Pat and headed to Shelter Island. I sat in the back of the car, cradling Monkey on my lap. For a while, she dozed. When she opened her dark little eyes, I noticed something on the lower lid of one of them. A wart? A pimple? Why hadn't I noticed this at Pat's? I took a closer look. It was a tick. It sat too close to her eye for me to pluck it off, even if I could get her to keep still. I thought back to my poor, dear Rusty. My heart sank. What if this nasty bug had infected my puppy? Fortunately, we were going to pass an animal hospital on the way. It was Friday, and I knew they were busy, but I'd taken Mercury there the previous summer for a check-up, and I was hoping they'd remember me and treat Monkey. The waiting room harbored a variety of dogs, mostly shaggy mutts, along with a few cats in carrier cases. Meows and woofs played in the background like a movie soundtrack. I approached the desk and spoke to the receptionist. She told me it might take an hour or longer until a veterinarian could see us. From her tone, I knew she wanted to say, "Next time make an appointment." Just then I saw a vet emerge from the exam room. I walked over to her with Monkey in my arms, and quickly explained the problem. She took us inside, removed the tick, and within minutes we were on our way. There was no charge.

Besides Rusty, Monkey was the only female puppy I'd had, and I really didn't remember anything about Rusty's puppyhood. That's why I took little Monkey upstairs and plunked her down on the bed. I was teasing her with my fingers, when suddenly she took a few steps forward and assumed a pose that resembled a duck landing on a pond. She peed. It was a puppy-sized puddle so it didn't go through to the mattress. As for the summer blanket and sheets, they were washable.

The next day, I took Monkey to Shelter Island's annual Blessing of the Pets, the very event Mercury had attended the year before. People kept coming up and asking what kind of dog she was. Like most folks, these admirers never had heard of a Schipperke. In addition to getting blessed, pets vied for awards, usually a ribbon, in such categories as the biggest nose, the best tail wagger, the oldest cat or dog, etc. That morning, Monkey won first place as "the smallest dog," and our picture appeared in the Shelter Island newspaper.

Bruce and I fawned over Monkey. She was alert, feisty and adorable, in sum, everything a Schipperke puppy should be. She was also related to Mercury, with the same "mommy," Gidget, but a different "daddy." Even at this early age, Monk had the attitude and spark of a winner. But then I noticed her bite. Her lower jaw jutted out ever so slightly, giving her what dog people call "bulldog mouth." Monkey had been so small when we first got her that neither of us had noticed this. Perhaps Pat hadn't either. But now, it was almost the end of summer, and Monkey was almost four months old. The official standard for the breed described the desired bite as follows: it must be scissors or level. Any deviation is to be severely penalized. I knew what that meant. In a ring full of Schipperkes at a dog show, a judge would immediately pass over my Monkey. "Severely penalized" translated to "fuhgedaboutit."

I called Pat. She reassured me somewhat by telling me that young puppies' mouths sometimes shift as they develop, and that it was possible Monkey's bite would adjust within the next few months. She also said I could return her. I suspect breeders say that all the time, knowing that only the most fervid seekers of show dogs would ever consider that option. We certainly didn't.

In September, when we went back to the city, I took Monkey to my veterinarian so he could examine her mouth. She definitely was undershot, but he suggested I take her to a canine dental specialist to find out if perhaps her bite would correct itself over time. Naturally, such a specialist could only be found at the Animal Medical Center. I wasn't eager to go there. The place held too many memories of Mercury. But in the fall of 1994, it was the only choice.

I don't recall exactly what this doggy dentist did to reach his conclusion, but he informed us that Monkey's bite was not going to change. People looking at her might never have noticed those little white teeth poking out from her lower jaw, but a judge certainly would have. Friends joked that perhaps I should get her braces. I suppose there are people who might have done that. Anything is possible in New York City if you have the money. But it wasn't cost that dissuaded me. It was the knowledge that Monkey had the wrong bite for her breed. That wasn't something I'd want her to pass on if she became a champion and was therefore available as a brood bitch. The whole idea behind breeding purebred dogs is that each litter should represent a betterment of that breed. Of course, no one can achieve perfection, but in theory, that's what breeders strive towards.

Monkey quickly learned to do her business outside. Every morning I took her to the park, always on lead. This was another lesson I'd learned from Mercury: no off-leash privileges. I'll never forget that day on Shelter Island when he took off and headed towards the road. I bought a Flexilead® so Monk could have 16 feet of running space and still be under my control.

In January, we had Monkey spayed. Though Schipperke puppies are among the cutest sights on earth, I had no intention of breeding her. I firmly believed, and still do, that breeding dogs is best left to those who take it seriously, who study genetics, who weed out health problems, and who devote the years necessary to gain thorough knowledge of their chosen breed. Though I was still trying to find something worthwhile to do in my middle years, I immediately knew this was too much work for me. I scratched "dog breeder" as a possible mid-life career.

January is one of the grayest months of winter in New York. It's a time when depressed people feel more depressed, and it's a time when everyone in the city seems gloomy. In my case, I still was nagged by depression. I had thought, or hoped, that Monkey would somehow make me feel uplifted and cheery, that her very presence would remove the dark weight that had settled inside me. But this was too big a job for a little Schipperke. I needed professional help. I called my doctor and asked him for Prozac. My husband and I also decided to see a marriage counselor. Ours was a strange relationship. It wasn't marred by daily fights or squabbles. In fact, there wasn't much vocalizing of any kind, only a sense of floating away from one another, like feathers on the wind, and a quiet seething about the other person's annoying habits.

There was one area though, where I couldn't keep silent. It concerned old newspapers. Bruce kept reams of them stacked on the coffee table in the living room. They were an eyesore and a potential *chateau* for silverfish. He'd already filled up the den, which served as his office, and I resented his messing up the rest of the apartment with what I considered debris. To make matters worse, he had furnished this den with an enormous roll top desk. It took up one third of the room, robbing me, I'd tell him time after time, of living space. But whenever I complained, he ignored me. I began to feel that old newspapers and his over-sized desk meant more to him than I did. The first counselor we saw said that if he were in that situation, he would throw out the newspapers and get a smaller desk, if these items made his wife unhappy. I liked him immediately. But right after that visit, Bruce's firm changed health insurers, and we had to change counselors. Unfortunately, this fellow wasn't on their list. This pleased my husband. Now he could keep his newspapers and offensive furniture, at least for a while. Our next counselor was young woman, probably just out of school, and of a different ethnicity than we. I wondered how well she'd relate to us, two middle-aged, marriage-weary New Yorkers whose problems probably disappointed her. We were not text book cases where adultery, abuse, drug addiction or shoplifting caused spouses to hate one another. I don't recall the details of our session, it was a long time ago, but I do remember the aftermath. When my husband and I left her office, we looked at each other and shook our heads. Therapy wasn't for us.

Some people might ask why we didn't divorce, but the truth is, he wasn't a bad person, just a pack rat, a fan of estate-sized furniture, and a clam. And this latter flaw was a big problem. Humans need companionship and someone to talk to, but with him, it was like living in a vacuum. After we'd seen a movie together, for example, we'd walk out without saying a word. I'd eavesdrop on other couples who were discussing the film. Finally I'd break the silence and ask if he liked the movie. I'd get a one word answer. On the plus side, he had style. He'd never order a Coke™ to accompany dinner in a fine restaurant. We always drank wine. Nor would he cover a platter of oysters with cocktail sauce, when *mignonette* was the better choice. And then, of course, there was the matter of the apartment. He wasn't about to give it up since it was his to begin with, and that meant, if we divorced, I'd have no place to go. We're both native New Yorkers with very parochial tastes. While some folks might consider moving to Brooklyn or Queens, or even to New Jersey, I had to be where I was—across the street from Central Park, in a pre-war building with two apartments to a floor and a doorman. Besides, the apartment was rent controlled.

After a few months, the Prozac started working for me. Dark moods vanished like morning dew. So did the range of my feelings. Now I was balanced but numb. Yet I rather liked my new state. Nothing upset me. Nothing elated me, except for my Monkey. She was smart and sassy, and already knew the command "sit," plus she was housebroken. I decided to train her in Obedience. For that AKC discipline, a dog or bitch needn't adhere to the standard. In fact, a lot of purebred dogs end up being trained for obedience titles because they have a conformation flaw or two.

Performance events such as Obedience and Agility take place at a "trial," not a "show," and for someone training a Schipperke as opposed to a breed that lives to please its owner, such as a Golden Retriever, the word "trial" was an understatement. Monk had a mind of her own, which became apparent once we entered competitions. To earn the novice title, CD, or Companion Dog, the first step in a series of increasingly challenging Obedience events, Monkey had to qualify with a score of 170 or better at three different trials, under three different judges. Each win was known as a leg, which made for strange remarks among competitors, such as "My dog has two legs." To those not in the know, this might've evoked an expression of sympathy. To Monkey, and who can really know what went through her canine mind, this could've meant, "Who cares?"

To try for a qualifying score, a dog had to perform a series of specific exercises: heel on lead and off, at both slow and fast gaits, sit and stay for one minute, then lie down and not move for three minutes, and come when called. It had to stand for examination, which meant letting the judge run his or her hands over its body, lightly and quickly. The dog also had to thread its way in heel position around two posts in a figure eight pattern. The "posts" were ring stewards who stood ramrod straight, six feet apart, with not a hint of a smile on either of their faces.

I had read the requirements for the CD title in a flyer I'd received from the American Kennel Club. The exercises seemed straightforward and simple, so I called the dog school where I'd taken Mercury for show handling classes. I was in luck. They offered Obedience, and there was a basic class beginning in October. If Monkey mastered the exercises, and if I trained her well, we'd be on our way to our first AKC title, Companion Dog.

Chapter 8

"Hey, Monk, Are You Ready for Dog School?"

Back then, Obedience candidates had to wear a buckle collar, not a choke, so Mercury's show lead remained in the closet. For Monkey, I bought a tan, rolled leather collar with brass hardware and a matching six foot lead. It was expensive but worth it. The collar looked great against her dark coat.

Anna didn't bring her Doberman to these classes, which meant Monk and I had to travel by bus. At the time, we lived on Fifth Avenue at 101st Street, so this wasn't a problem. Of the four bus lines that stopped across from my building, two of them went straight down to 23rd Street. From there, it was a two block walk west to the dog school. Before the first class, I practiced luring Monkey into her Sherpa® bag. I'd learned my lesson with Mercury. One Friday morning in the spring of his second year, I was driving to Shelter Island. I needed to stop at the Department of Motor Vehicles in Riverhead to turn in license plates from a car we'd sold. Mercury always traveled in a crate, as do all my small dogs, but it was warm and sunny that day, and I wasn't about to leave him in the car. Earlier in the week, I'd bought a Sherpa® bag just for this errand. I took him out of his crate, put on his lead and headed towards the DMV building. There was a small area between the two sets of glass doors, and I figured this was a perfect spot to put him into the bag. Only he wouldn't go. I tried to stuff him in it, but he kept wiggling out. He stiffened his legs so he wouldn't fit. Inside, a woman at the Information desk watched us. Finally, I got him in and quickly zipped the bag. I entered the facility and asked this woman on which line I needed to wait. She was smiling, which is most unusual for a government employee. She said I needn't have put him in the bag. He could've come in as long as he was on a leash. Times have changed and I'm sure that's no longer the case, but I remember being ticked that I'd spent money for a bag I didn't need. With Monkey, I took no chances. First I showed her the bag. Then I paved the way inside with liver treats. She quickly ate the treat at the open end, then stretched herself till she resembled an otter in an attempt to get the other snacks. She had no desire to plunge head first into that dark "tunnel." Finally, greed took over and she entered the bag, devouring the remaining treats. After a few rounds of this, she decided that the Sherpa® bag was a good place to hang out.

I soon discovered there was more to Obedience than training the dog. The handler needed instruction as well. For example, in a 180 degree change of direction, known as the "about turn," the person holding the lead needed to place his or her feet *just so* in order to turn around fluidly without dragging the dog. People with Golden Retrievers and other large breeds had an advantage. During training, they could keep their dog's attention by popping treats in its mouth with every step. Small dog owners had to hunch over or attach a treat to a stick to obtain the same result. Of course, at official Obedience trials, treats were *verboten*, but in class they worked wonders.

I practiced with Monkey in the park and in front of our building. One of the trickiest parts of Obedience at the Novice level is to keep the dog's attention. Distractions abound at a trial, whether it's another dog barking near the ring, a little kid crying, or the sudden roar of a motorcycle starting up in the parking lot. Monkey, a city girl, was used to all kinds of noise. Buses, trucks, honking horns, these sounds were background music to her ears. As we did with Mercury, my husband and I often took her to outdoor cafes with us when the weather was nice. This was another way to get her comfortable with potential distractions. She'd lie down under the table or sit by my chair. Passers-by, of course, couldn't resist asking about her. One warm autumn day, we drove downtown to the Odeon, a restaurant with outdoor seating. There was a parking space right in front, and an empty table on the patio, two things that rarely occur in the same place in our city. Before we even sat down, I noticed the couple at the next table. It was the late John Kennedy and his lovely wife-to-be, Carolyn Bessette. Their dog, Friday, reclined at John's feet. Monkey, of course, had to say "hi" to Friday, and Friday to her. John nodded and asked my dog's name, and I asked him his. Then he returned to reading his newspaper, while Carolyn drank her coffee.

I reined in Monkey and placed her alongside me. Bruce, who definitely needed more exposure to gossip columns and celebrity magazines, said, a bit too loudly, "Who's that? He looks familiar."

Out of the side of my mouth, I told him. Then we ordered. Soon, a tourist arrived with a camera and asked if she could take John's picture. He shook his head. His Sunday brunch ruined, he put money on the table. Then he, Carolyn and Friday got up and left. As I watched them cross the street, the "Mercury" hubcap in that magazine photo of Jackie popped into my mind. Now Mercury's half-sister, Monkey, had made her own connection with the Kennedys.

We finished our food and headed back uptown. Monkey loved to ride in the car, and on short hops around the city, I didn't use the crate. She'd stand on my lap and look out the window, her dark eyes flitting back and forth, taking in the action on the streets. She was beautiful, even with that bad bite. I'd put off calling Pat Nigey to tell her the dentist's final conclusion. It was a touchy situation. We had paid a show dog price for Monkey, and of course, to us, she was worth every cent. But I had wanted a show dog, a dog who could finish Mercury's quest and get to the Garden. Unfortunately for me, Monkey wasn't it. I don't know what I'd hoped to gain by telling Pat the final results of the dental consultations. I doubted she would offer to refund some of our money. But I decided to call her anyway.

Chapter 9

The Odyssey Begins

Pat was apologetic about Monkey's bite, but as I suspected, offered no rebate. She told me a pup had been born out of Mercury's half-sister the past spring. She was sure he was show quality, and had kept him this long to see how he'd develop. His littermate had died at birth, so he was what dog people called a "singleton." These pups often have personality problems unless the breeder takes an active hand in playing with them and socializing them. Pat thought this puppy had turned out all right. He was, at this time, seven months old.

It rained torrents the day we drove to Pat's. This meant we couldn't play with the pup outside. I remember spending the entire time in Pat's kitchen. When I first saw this dog, I thought to myself, he's awfully skinny and long in the back. I was still new to the world of show dogs in general, and Schipperkes in particular, so I failed to see his promise. I voiced my hesitation out loud. Pat said he was young and that he'd fill out. I wasn't sure I believed her, but I said that we'd take him. Pat mentioned a price that was more than we'd paid for Monkey, and although I wanted this puppy, both Bruce and I balked. A few awkward moments ensued. Finally we negotiated a price that was less than we'd paid for Monkey, but somewhat more than what we'd paid for Mercury. I looked at my husband and told him to write Pat a check. Then I put the leash on my new puppy. He had a mission. Like Jason seeking the Golden Fleece on his ship, Argo, this dog had to go to the Garden to complete Mercury's odyssey. I filled out the registration papers. Name: Kebrill's Mercurial Argonaut.

We had prepared Monkey for the new pup's arrival by telling her she was going to have a brother. Actually, we told her she was going to have a puppy, as in a canine immaculate conception. We'd set up a wire crate with a soft cushion in the bedroom. Monkey circled it daily, sniffing it, checking for signs of this newcomer. When we came home with Argo, I told my husband to wait in the foyer with him. Monkey greeted me at the door. Then we let Argo in. Monk chased him down our long hallway, and the two of them whirled about, jumping and running like hedgehogs on amphetamines. At that time I didn't know the right way to introduce dogs to each other—on neutral territory, on lead—but this worked out fine. Monkey and Argo became lifelong buddies, and I finally found my mid-life calling—dog mother.

Monkey finished dog school in December, and all the "students" passed their final exam—a mock Obedience trial. In the spring, I planned to enter her in Novice A at any match or trial within three hours driving distance, the same limit I'd set with Mercury. But this time there would be no hired handler. Obedience trials and all the other performance dog sports—Agility, Rally, Utility, Tracking—were designed to show the bond between human and dog. In most cases, the humans were the owners. These events also provided a fun way to spend a Saturday or Sunday with one's pooch. I discovered, too, that most AKC trials were held in conjunction with AKC Conformation shows, which meant shopping opportunities at a variety of vendor booths for such goodies as dog themed clothing, toys, beds, leashes, collars, and knick knacks.

Meanwhile, Argo had settled in, and although Pat had assured me he was house trained, he occasionally surprised me with unspeakable behavior. I remember one particular morning. I was in the bedroom, putting on my sneakers, getting ready to take out the dogs. Argo looked up at me as if to say, "Wait till you see what I have for you."

Then he squatted and pooped right there on the rug. Was this a canine version of a housewarming gift? "Dirty dog," I said as he lowered his head and skulked past the pile. Monkey, hearing the commotion, trotted in and quickly put on the brakes. She sniffed the air, then spotted the offensive offering. I never thought a dog could show disdain, but that's definitely the expression I saw on her face. She turned and quickly left the room.

In May, I took Monkey to an Obedience match. It was outside on a sunny day. Luckily it wasn't hot. When the temperature rises, black coated dogs tend to absorb more heat than their lighter colored cousins. This quickly can lead to heatstroke. That's why I always carried a spray bottle of cold water to outdoor shows so I could keep Monk cool. She'd let me soak her, then she'd shake off and soak me right back.

On that particular day, Monkey seemed eager for new adventures. Since this was a match, not a trial, there were no "legs" at stake. Even if there were, Monkey wouldn't have earned any. She was fascinated by the goings on around her. When the judge called my number, we entered the ring, and Monkey sat nicely in heel position on my left. I looked straight ahead, ready to step out the moment the judge said, "Forward." In those few seconds, I took my eyes off Monkey, giving her the opportunity to swivel out of position and observe the people at ringside. On the judge's command, I moved but Monkey didn't. In fact, when I advanced, the lead grew taut, and Monkey, glued to where she was sitting, almost tipped over. I looked at the judge. A smile played at her lips. For the long sit, Monk was positioned between a Cocker Spaniel and a Rottweiler. In Obedience, any of the recognized AKC breeds may be found in the ring at the same time. I looked at the Rottweiler and so did Monkey. His head was bigger than her entire body. When the judge called for us to leave our dogs and move to the other side of the ring, I was half way across when I heard chuckling. I turned around. Monkey was right behind me. I put her back in place and the judge told me to attach the lead and stay with her for the one minute sit, and also for the three minute down. I was grateful. I didn't want my little girl becoming a snack for that Rottie. In my book, *Schipperkes. A Complete Pet Owner's Manual*, published by Barron's Educational Series Inc. in 1998, there is a picture of Monkey at this Obedience match. It's on page 69, and if ever there was a dog who could care less about following the rules, it was Miss Monkey.

In those early days of Obedience outings, Argo stayed home with my husband. They probably watched football or basketball together, I don't really know. But when Monk and I returned home, Argo was always at the door to greet us. In time, I would enter shows that had both Obedience and Breed competitions, and the three of us—Monkey, Argo and I—would head off in the car together. Bruce stayed home. Though he loved our dogs, he hated dog shows. He also disliked, but not hated, the responsibilities that came with having dogs—walking them in the rain, taking them to the vet, finding someone to watch them when vacations came up, and maintaining a consistent level of training. Most of this fell upon me, but I didn't mind. I was, after all, a dog mother.

At these trials, and later at shows with Argo, I met people who expressed surprise that I lived in New York City and had two dogs. They wondered how I managed. It was easy. We lived across the street from Central Park, so it was convenient for walking. Every morning, except when it rained, Monkey, Argo and I trekked around the reservoir, a hike of a little over a mile. Sometimes we investigated the northern end of the park at the Harlem Meer, where ducks and geese roamed freely in a nature preserve setting. Argo enjoyed chasing these birds to the end of his 16 foot retractable lead, but even more, he loved eating goose poop. He was quick and sneaky, often grabbing a piece before I could rein him in. Other times we dropped down into the woodlands where there was a bog, a stream and a waterfall that rushed over the rocks. On the other side of a stone bridge, a short distance away, stood the Lasker Ice Skating Rink. In winter, the residue from the Zamboni's clean-up was piled outside the rink. I'd ask the Schippies, "Who likes ice?" and they'd charge over towards the mounds and climb to the top as if scaling a mini Mt. Everest. Sometimes they dug holes in the snow, and sometimes they ate it.

This area of the park had been extremely dangerous back in the days before Mayor Giuliani. Then, thanks to an increased police presence and the efforts of the Central Park Conservancy, the drug dealers and derelicts were kicked out, and a major beautification and clean-up effort materialized. The park was heaven for dogs. They were allowed off the leash between nine at night and nine in the morning. They could run, chase each other, retrieve Frisbees® and get all the exercise they needed for the day. At night, though, it was still tricky. There was a footpath inside the park, directly across from our apartment building, and I'd walk Monkey and Argo there for their last walk of the day, usually around nine or nine-thirty. I always kept my eyes open, scanning the huge boulders that rose above the walkway like a miniature mountain range. Shadowy figures often smoked, and probably sold, marijuana up there, but they never bothered me and the dogs. One night though, a man carrying an enormous plastic bag filled with cans suddenly appeared at the head of the stairs that led to this path. He was one of the homeless who emptied trash bins in order to redeem cans and bottles for the 5 cent deposit that New York State imposed. The moment Argo saw him, his scruff went up and he started barking. Though small, he looked scary, especially in the dark, when only his large white teeth glistened under the lamplight. Monkey joined the barkfest. The man blocked the path, and we couldn't safely get around him. Suddenly he raised his bag of cans and moved it back and forth like a scythe. He said he was going to kill my dogs. That's all I needed to hear. I quickly turned around and headed deeper into the park. The walkway descended towards another set of stairs, past a playground, and finally to an exit. We made it home without further problems, and the next night, we were back on "our" path, unfazed.

Sometimes though, trouble erupted inside our building. There was one tenant whose wife feared these two little Schipperkes. Once, she was already in the elevator when it opened on our floor. She saw the dogs and recoiled against the elevator wall. I told her we'd wait. Obviously she didn't realize that Monkey and Argo were perfect city dogs. They never barked at respectable people or tried to jump on them. That's why I was incensed one evening as I was taking them out for a walk. When the elevator doors opened on the ground floor, a man loomed in our path. I stifled a scream. The Schips barked and lunged. Clearly they thought this fellow was a menace because nobody with good manners stands right in front of the elevator. The man dropped the pile of papers he was carrying. He made a remark about the dogs, and I don't remember what it was, but I do recall telling him that he scared *me*.

He was the husband of the woman who was afraid of Monkey and Argo. He was also a doctor at Mt. Sinai Hospital, which happened to own our apartment building. He wrote a letter to the Real Estate Department, demanding that I take my dogs out via the back elevator. This elevator, also known as the service elevator, is used to transport garbage to the basement, which the porter picks up daily. Unlike the front elevator, it wasn't automated so I would have had to ring for someone to come up and get me and the dogs. That meant we'd have to wait, and then travel in less than first class style. I found this unacceptable, especially since we'd lived in the building much longer than this complainer. There were other doctors living there at that time, and two of them had dogs. I wrote back to the Real Estate manager, explaining that I would gladly use the service elevator as long as Dr. X and Dr. Y did so as well. I never heard another word about this, and the Schips and I continued to take the front elevator. One day, shortly before this doctor and his wife moved out of the building and out of the state, I noticed her in our local, dog friendly bookstore. Monkey and Argo were with me. When she saw us, she fled.

Another tenant took a much more cheerful approach. He told me he had allergies. Whenever I saw him in the elevator, I'd let him go and take the next one. If we met him in the lobby, he gave us wide berth. But he always had a smile on his face.

Lillian, my neighbor, adored Monkey and Argo. She was a widow in her nineties, living in a much larger apartment than ours, one that had fabulous views of the park, as well as a miniscule rent stabilized rent. The sprawling layout offered lots of space for two Schipperkes to romp. She had a live-in caregiver named June who took in our Saturday and Sunday newspapers whenever we went to Shelter Island for the weekend. On Sunday nights when we returned, I'd bring them something—flowers from the garden, a pumpkin at Halloween, or vegetables from one of the farm stands that abound on the North Fork of Long Island. I'd always call first, and the moment I picked up the phone, Monkey and Argo started whining with anticipation. They twirled around and zoomed to the door, scratching at it like prisoners bent on escape. Then, they scampered across the marble floor of the small foyer that separated our apartments, and began scratching at Lillian's door. The moment June opened it, they charged past her and dashed inside, inspecting every room as if seeing it for the first time. Then, they'd visit Lillian. She loved to dig her bony, arthritic fingers into the dogs' thick fur and gently scratch them. This was our weekend routine for many years. As time passed, Lillian grew frail, and developed dementia, but her eyes lit up each time Monkey and Argo came bounding into her apartment. When she died, she was 102.

Monkey and Argo had definite likes and dislikes. There was a woman in our neighborhood who had two Chihuahuas. She brought them to the park every morning, and in cool weather, dressed them in colorful sweaters and coats. To this day, I don't know whether Monkey loathed their taste in fashion or just disliked them as dogs, but every time she saw them, she'd rush to the end of her Flexi Lead® and bark like a rabid coyote. Argo had no interest in these little dogs or in Monkey's crazed antics. He focused on sniffing the ground and marking his territory. I soon realized I could turn Monk's feelings about these Chihuahuas into a people pleasing stunt. I began to condition her. Every time we saw those dogs, I'd say, "Chi . . . chi chi chi. Chihuahua." She'd growl and bark. Eventually, indoors, I could elicit the same reaction.

Argo, on the other hand, hated certain breeds of big dogs. He was fine with Great Danes, for example, but he could spot a Pit Bull or a Rottweiler from several blocks away. Immediately his scruff went up and he tugged at the lead. "Let me at 'em," his posture said. He had a deep bark, and I often remarked, that anyone coming to our door who didn't know Argo, would think there was a Doberman Pinscher or a German Shepherd Dog inside. Sometimes I wished he were one. Then risky situations wouldn't frighten me as much as this one did. A woman around the corner from our apartment building had a Pit Bull named Platinum. For the most part, I like Pit Bulls, but this dog looked mean. His eyes were so light, they appeared translucent, making him seem eerie, like a zombie in a horror film. Plus, he wasn't neutered. People in the park who knew him, said he had attacked several dogs when he was off lead. Whenever Argo saw him and he saw Argo, they'd growl and lunge at each other, pulling at their leashes. Platinum's owner was short, like me, and she could barely hold onto him. One day, on our way back after a jaunt around the reservoir, I saw Platinum in the distance near the path we took to get home. He was off the leash. Suddenly, he started trotting towards us. I called to the woman to get him. Perhaps she didn't hear me, because she paid no attention. Soon, Argo and

Platinum were nose to nose. I had dropped Monkey's leash and told her to stay. Thank heavens for that Obedience training. The two males circled each other, hackles up. In another minute, I was sure Platinum would to attack. I pulled out a length of Flexi Lead® and twirled it like a garrotte. I told the woman if she didn't take Platinum away immediately, I would choke him to death. She shooed him off, but couldn't catch him to leash him. We hurried home. From that day on, whenever she saw us, she quickly put him on lead and walked in the opposite direction. I'm sure she thought I was dangerous.

Chapter 10

The Odyssey Continues

In June 1996, a month after that Obedience match, I took the dogs to Shelter Island for the summer. The Animal Rescue Fund of the Hamptons (ARF) was offering weekly Obedience classes at their facility near the East Hampton airport, and I enrolled Monkey. It was a short ride from Shelter Island, including a five minute ferry crossing, and since summer hadn't officially started, I didn't have to worry about long ferry lines or traffic. Monkey loved riding in the car. All I had to say is, "Monk, are you ready for dog school?" and she'd twirl around, dash out the door, and hop into the front seat. Then I'd put her in the crate. Argo stayed home alone. Luckily, he wasn't a destructive dog so I didn't have to fret that he might chew the rattan furniture in the porch or unstuff a throw pillow.

Bruce came out on weekends, and took a short vacation in July. I was convinced his only purpose was to undo all the training I'd instilled in the dogs. Often, at dinner, I saw his hand slide from his plate down towards the floor, a tidbit clutched between his fingers. "Don't feed them from the table," I'd say. But he was like a bad child. He kept defying me, until one day I blew up. I was surprised that my Prozac-mellowed brain allowed such an outburst. I slammed my hand on the table, I yelled, I told him how hard I worked to train the dogs and how little respect he had for my efforts, and this led, naturally, to my pointing out his other shortcomings. It was a grand and glorious one-sided fight. He remained tight-lipped through it all. Over time, he devised other ways to funnel food to the dogs. For example, small pieces of meat often jumped from his plate to the floor while he cut his food. His napkin, moist with juice from a hamburger, slid off his lap to an open mouth and eager tongue. And sometimes, stopped by my glare, he got up, took a few tidbits and ambled into the kitchen. Monkey and Argo followed, noses tilted towards the ceiling, hoping for something to drop along the way. Opportunists to the core, whenever we sat down for a meal, the two Schippies always positioned themselves under the table, next to Bruce's chair.

His anti-training extended to other areas of canine behavior as well. Though Schipperkes are small, on their hind legs, they can reach two feet, or just the right height to put a snag in someone's stockings or silk skirt. That's why I trained Monkey and Argo to respond to the command, "off." They learned quickly, and never jumped on me, but they loved to jump on my husband. He let them, of course, and it made me crazy. "Just lift your knee and say, "off," I'd tell him. He'd do it under my gaze, as a peace-making gesture, but an hour later, I'd see Schipperkes hopping up and down, using his thighs as a springboard. Times like these made me want to put a choke collar on him and haul him off to dog school.

Despite my husband's negative impact on dog training, Monkey usually paid attention to me. Sometimes this meant increasing the volume of my voice when I gave the command, going from *piano* to *fortissimo*, and adding a "*Miss* Monkey" for emphasis. I often said this when I found her lounging on the glass coffee table on the porch at the Shelter Island house. This became her favorite resting spot throughout her entire life, no matter how many times I corrected her. Typical Monkey. She knew she wasn't supposed to lie there, yet her inner Schipperke said, "Go ahead, do it." Often as she grew older, I only had to stand in the doorway leading to the porch, my hands on my hips, and say, *Miss* Monkey." She'd hop off, for the moment, but later, she'd return to her perch, until I caught her again.

Every day, in the late afternoon during that summer, I held obedience sessions on the lawn. From time to time, Monkey heeled perfectly, showing me she knew what I wanted, but reminding me, as in the Rolling Stones's song, "You can't always get what you want," that I should prepare for disappointment. I worked on my own handling, too. I thought, wrongly as it turned out, that I'd finally gotten the knack of where I was supposed to put my feet when changing direction. During our sessions, Argo stayed inside, like an actor waiting in the wings, his nose pressed against the screen door. He may not have realized it, but he played an important role in Monkey's training. Like Arnold Schwarzenegger, who was famous as "The Terminator," before he was elected governor, Argo became "The Distractor." He was a natural. He didn't need an agent to get this important part, nor did he need rehearsals. I'd let him out while she was practicing the long "sit" or "down." First he'd run and mark some bushes. Then he'd come to me, hoping to get a treat. When Monkey saw this, she often broke her sit or down. She wasn't the type of girl who might pass up a chance to get food. It was a real challenge trying to put an Obedience title on this headstrong Schipperke because one never knew what to expect.

In the fall, I took her to her first Obedience trial. It was in Westchester, outdoors, on a sunny but cool day, perfect weather for a crisp, sure-footed performance. Only Monkey didn't qualify. She lagged behind in heeling, both on lead and off. Part of it was my fault. I still hadn't mastered the fluid foot placement that led to a flawless about turn. When we left the ring, I took her aside. "Monkey," I said, "look at those other doggies. Watch them and do better next time."

She looked at me as if to say, "If you wanted blind devotion, you should've gotten a Golden Retriever. If you wanted a dog that loved to follow rules, you should've bought a Doberman. Just remember, I'm a Schipperke, and it was *your* idea to try Obedience."

Then a woman took *me* aside. She belonged to the group sponsoring the trial, the Portchester Training and Obedience Club. She said they held classes during the day during the week, and a new class was starting in two weeks. This fit my schedule perfectly. She suggested I could use some help with my footwork. I thanked her. Actually, I was insulted. While I wasn't as smooth as some of the more adept women at this trial, I didn't think I'd come off as a bumbler. Clearly though, to outside observers, both Monkey and I needed help. On Monday morning, first thing, I called Portchester and registered Monk for the Novice A class. Unfortunately, this dog school wasn't a quick bus or taxi ride away.

My husband used his car to drive to work in New Jersey. He parked on the street and took off before parking restrictions began in the morning. My car stayed on Shelter Island. Sometimes I brought it to the city and parked in a garage that charged $20 a day, cheap by Manhattan standards, but no bargain if all the car did was sit there until it was time for a weekly excursion to the dog school. So Monkey and I traveled by public transportation. She knew the Sherpa® bag spelled adventure. When I took it out of the closet, she twirled and pranced like a hot-headed race horse. I'd attach her lead and we'd walk around the corner to Madison Avenue to wait for the #1 bus. Three other buses ran on this line, the #2, the #3 and the #4, so I let Monkey stand with me and the other passengers until the bus we needed arrived. Sometimes this took ten or fifteen minutes. Then I'd open the bag and say, "Monkey, go inside." As she went in and I zipped the bag, I noticed the people around me smiling. At 125th Street, we disembarked and I took her out of the bag. We walked two blocks to the Metro North station, past street vendors and shoppers. Everyone cast an admiring eye at Monkey, often asking her breed. Even derelicts, slumped in doorways, smiled as she trotted by. Then Monkey climbed back into the bag and we took the train to White Plains. From there, it was a twenty minute walk to the dog school. The neighborhood through which we passed was shabby and there was a lot of trash on the street, including empty liquor bottles and cans of Colt 45, yet no one ever bothered us, but, unlike the friendly people in Harlem, nobody ever asked about Monkey or stopped to tell me how beautiful she was. Dogs barked as we walked by, though I never saw them. They were inside the ramshackle houses, and thankfully, locked up. After class, we made the same trip in reverse. Luckily, even though it was winter, it never rained or snowed on the days we went to Portchester.

I had decided not to enter any more trials until Monkey finished her training. Unlike the people at the dog school in the city, who, for the most part took Obedience courses in order to end up with well-behaved pets, these folks were serious about competition. From their intensity and focus, and their choice of breeds eager to work or please, I was willing to bet each and every one of them would get Companion Dog titles on their dogs within three to five trials. With Monkey, it took thirteen.

My parents adored Monkey and I had already taken her by plane to visit them in Florida the previous year. She traveled in her bag tucked under the seat in front of mine, quiet as the proverbial mouse. This time, I decided to take Argo. There was a cluster of dog shows in Sarasota, a forty-five minute drive up the Interstate from my parent's home in Port Charlotte. These took place from January 8th through 12th which was perfect timing for me. This was right after Ukrainian Christmas on January 7th, one of the dates of my bi-annual visit. I figured that these conveniently scheduled shows would offer me a chance to put some points on Argo.

I had bought the largest size Sherpa® bag for Argo, after determining he couldn't fit into Monkey's. I used the same *Hansel and Gretel* technique I'd used with Monk, leaving a trail of tidbits that led into the dark interior. The first time he went inside, he stood, making the top of the bag form a mound, like a camel's hump. I realized this was never going to fit under an airplane seat, especially in coach. Clearly, more training was in order. Argo knew the command, "down," so I opened the front panel of the bag and had him lie down. The only problem was, I couldn't re-zip it. In the prone position, he was too long and his head stuck out. I gently pushed him backward, telling him, "Make yourself small." Although he was very handsome, he wasn't as bright as Monkey. It took a while, and a lot of pushing, but he finally figured out that he had to curl up like a cat in order to fit. When he did, I dropped a treat through the top and again said, "Make yourself small." Whenever I flew with either Monkey or Argo, I always took a window seat. Once we took off and were in the air, I'd unzip the front panel and let the Schipperke stick its nose out. Both dogs were great travelers, like Mercury.

My parents came to the first show of the cluster on January 8th. The weather was great, sunny but not too hot, with low humidity. My parents were both in their early eighties at that time, and I was afraid a day outdoors might overwhelm them. But they seemed to enjoy looking at all the different breeds of dogs. My dad saw a Black and Tan Coonhound, which he thought was a Doberman Pinscher with floppy ears and a tail. When he "complimented" its owner, he received a cool rebuke. My mom enjoyed making snide remarks about the tubby women handlers who wore the most colorful, bold floral print skirts she'd ever seen. She said, a little too loudly, as one of them waddled by with her Bulldog, "Look at that, she looks just like her dog." I was glad I didn't know any of the people at this show.

After a few hours, though, my folks got bored. Not surprisingly, they declined my invitation to come to the remaining shows. Perhaps it was because their "grandson" hadn't won any ribbons. Again, a lot of this was my fault. I was so busy training Monkey that I hadn't practiced enough with Argo. He needed to learn to stand still on the table so the judge could feel his structure, and of course, his testicles. Anna could help me with this when I returned to the city, but if she weren't available, I had no Plan B. I couldn't imagine going up to a stranger on the street and asking him or her to please run their hands over my dog and check his nuts.

As I looked at the other Schipperkes in the ring that day, I had to admit that Argo appeared rather skinny compared to the cobbier, more full-coated three year-old dog that took the points. I remembered what one judge had told me about Mercury, to put a little weight on him and let him grow up. Too bad I hadn't applied her advice to Argo. Yet I wasn't ready to quit. I'd paid for three more shows in this cluster, so I decided to use them for practice. And maybe, just maybe, I'd get lucky. Unfortunately for me, the results were the same: no points for Argo.

Chapter 11

The Monkey Trials

Dog shows come to a screeching halt in February to make way for the "Academy Awards" of the canine world, The Westminster Kennel Club Dog Show. It's our country's longest continuously running sporting event, after the Kentucky Derby. The dog show started in 1877, the Derby in 1875. Back in the early days, the breeds we know and love today didn't compete. This was a real sportsmen's event with the emphasis on hunting dogs. That's why the Pointer was chosen as Westminster's logo. The club itself was named after the hotel where the men gathered, in the bar, to regale one another with tales of their shooting adventures. In time, the group expanded as more people became interested in showing their dogs. Westminster's website, *www.westminsterkennelclub.org* provides a fascinating history of the show's evolution, and it's worth checking out.

After the Florida cluster, I had to wait until March to find a show in our area. I don't think Argo minded the break. He seemed perfectly happy to hang out at home with Monkey or to chase deer with her on Shelter Island. Those deer, some as big as horses, ate our lawn for breakfast and our shrubs for dinner. Whenever I spotted them, I opened the door and said, "Bambi!" Monkey and Argo, whining with excitement, zoomed out, side by side, like a furry black missiles, and chased them away. Then they feasted on deer poop. One time, though, a deer stood its ground. It was a doe with a fawn nearby. Suddenly the two Schipperkes put on the brakes. Clearly, something was wrong here. The deer was *supposed* to flee at the sight of them charging up the hill. Still barking, they edged backward, unsure what to do. A fawn soon emerged from the bushes. It teetered on thin, gangly legs, then, spotting its mother, broke into a trot. The dogs watched, but didn't advance. The doe led it away, hopping over a fence into our neighbor's yard and to safety.

Vacationing on Shelter Island was fun for the dogs, but Argo had a mission, and it wasn't to earn a title as the best deer chaser in town. He had to get to the Garden, for Mercury. Despite our poor showing in Florida, I felt optimistic. I entered him in the Riverhead Kennel Club dog show on March 30th. This time, I checked the judging program. If I had seen the name of that thin-lipped fellow who had treated me shabbily when I first showed Mercury, I would've stayed home.

In a small spiral notebook, I kept notes on all my dogs' shows and trials. If it weren't for that, I never would have remembered how events unfolded. At Riverhead, Argo won no points. Krista was there with one of her Specials, and he went Best of Breed. Krista was a face that judges recognized, plus she always had good-looking Schipperkes at the end of her lead. I asked her if she would show Argo for me. A couple of weeks later, she took him to a show in Virginia and he came home with a three point major.

Meanwhile, Monkey and I were getting ready to fly to Washington State for the Schipperke Club of America's National Specialty. This is an annual gathering of breeders and fanciers, held in different parts of the country, hosted by one of the regional clubs. In addition to Conformation classes of every category known to dogdom, there's also Obedience and sometimes Agility. The event lasts several days. I'd entered Monkey in Novice A, figuring she'd qualify with ease. There were no Rottweilers, Dobermans or other big dogs to scare her. She'd compete with her own kind.

In the past, Monkey had flown to Florida with me, but a cross country flight was a bigger test of her airplane manners. I couldn't imagine keeping her zipped in her bag and stuffed under the seat in front of me for five and a half hours. In those pre-9/11 days, flying was actually fun. There were no TSA agents scrutinizing everything from aspirins to shampoo, and flight attendants wore genuine smiles. No one was going to object to Monkey. She was my carry-on bag, and of course I didn't pay for her. I wore a black pantsuit, perfect for camouflaging a little black dog. And I chose the window seat. The middle seat was empty, and a woman sat on the aisle. I asked her if she had any problems with dogs, and when she said, no, I took Monk out of the bag and put her on my lap. She stayed there for the entire trip, except during meal service, when I placed her on the empty seat, "camouflaged" by my suit jacket. I knew the flight attendant saw her, but as I said, this was back in the good old days.

My brother from Seattle planned to stop by the show and spend some time with me. I invited him to see the Novice A competition. This was Monkey's first indoor show, and although the rubber mats on the floor provided the same familiar footing as Portchester, that's where similarities ended. Here, there were spectators, dozens of them. They'd brought their own chairs and plunked them down alongside the ring with their bags, which probably contained snacks that Monkey could smell. The room itself was huge and later would serve as the banquet hall for the dinner the last night of the Specialty. Monkey and I entered the ring. She sat perfectly on my left, and took a few steps with me when the judge said, "Forward." Then I felt the leash tighten. I turned to see Monkey trying to squeeze through the accordion gate that surrounded the ring. A spectator was eating a muffin, and Monk figured she could snag a few crumbs. I brought her back to heel and we continued with the on-lead exercises. When it came time to heel free, it was clear Monkey had ideas of her own. If she could speak, she might've said, "Mom, you are free to heel all over this place, but I have other plans. See ya'." And so I found myself halfway around the ring, alone. Laughter had erupted on the sidelines, and one of the voices I recognized belonged to my brother. I looked back to see Monkey lying down, or should I say *lounging* on the mat a few yards from the point where we'd started. The steward handed me my lead and told me to go get her. We didn't qualify.

When we returned home, I entered Monkey in an Obedience trial on Staten Island. Meanwhile, Argo went out with Krista again and came home with another three point major. I was thrilled, and even my husband, who groused somewhat good-naturedly about the money I was spending on dog shows, seemed proud. Now it was Monkey's turn to show a return on investment. I was hoping this upcoming trial would give her her first leg. Staten Island, though part of New York City, is unknown territory to most Manhattanites. I was among them. As soon as I crossed the Verrazano Bridge, I took a wrong turn and spent twenty minutes trying to find the high school where the dog show and trials were held. I had a map and written directions, but somehow the street signs on Staten Island came up too fast or tilted the wrong way, so I often overshot the road I needed. This probably didn't bother Monkey. She preferred riding in the car to heeling around a ring.

The Obedience ring was in a walled-off area at one end of the school's gym. There were few spectators, since most of the people who had come to the show were focused on the Conformation classes. No distractions, I thought, as I began to picture Monkey receiving her ribbon after qualifying. But then I saw the Novice A dogs. There were all big, with two representatives of our "favorite" breed, Rottweiler. I prayed that Monkey wouldn't get stuck between them for the sits and downs. When we entered the ring, Monk kept looking at these big guys and gals, standing on the sidelines, awaiting their turns to compete. I could tell she was nervous. She didn't sit when I halted, and once again, she let me heel by myself when I removed the lead. At least this time, she didn't lie down on the job, she just moseyed along several feet behind me. I don't recall where she was positioned for sits and downs, but I do remember that two dogs started a scuffle. Suddenly, all the dogs erupted in an earsplitting blast of growls and barks. Monkey looked left, then right, then left again, unsure how to escape the melee. I rushed to her and scooped her up. I could feel her heart racing. "It's o.k., Monk," I said, "we're out of here." I told the judge we were withdrawing. It didn't matter. Monkey wouldn't have qualified anyway.

There are people who can train Schipperkes to do amazing things. When I was at the Specialty, I saw Schips vying for the CDX title (Companion Dog Excellent) where they had to leap over a high jump and retrieve a dumbbell, as well as fly over a broad jump in another part of the exercise. I witnessed Schips working towards their UD (Utility Dog) which entailed scent discrimination. The dog had to find the handler's scent from among a batch of approved articles spread out on the mat. These articles, made of metal and leather were not as easy to detect as an owner's smelly socks, for example. I also met a woman who did Search and Rescue with her Schipperkes. Her dogs could sniff out murder victims buried in the woods or find survivors at disaster sites amidst rubble that bigger dogs couldn't penetrate. When she showed me a souvenir bone from one of the cadavers her dogs had unearthed, I had new respect for the breed. Clearly, Schipperkes were trainable, despite their independent nature. So what was it with Miss Monkey?

I knew she was attached to me. At night, I used two pillows, and Monkey slept on the one I placed above my head. In the morning, if I dared sleep past the time she wanted to get up and have breakfast, she'd tap me on the head with her paw. She never slept on my husband's side of the bed. Neither did Argo. He had a "cave," under a lamp table in the bedroom. It was furnished with an old muskrat coat I'd bought at a flea market for $10. I loved both these dogs. Yet sometimes I thought it might've been better to have only one. Perhaps Monkey would have been more attuned to Obedience if I had spent extra time with her and hadn't had to pay attention to Argo as well.

More and more, I thought of Monkey and Argo as *my* dogs. Sure, they liked my husband, he'd bribe them with treats, but they listened to me. I walked them, I fed them, I groomed them every day, and I wiped their butts. Actually, that was Argo's problem, not Monkey's. He often made soft stools, and the hair around his anus got soiled. "Dirty poopies" or "deepees" was the name I gave his predicament. I'd clean him off with the flea comb and water. It didn't bother me one bit.

Monkey loved to chase and retrieve her small latex soccer ball when I tossed it down the hall and cried, "Soccer ball." I'd let my husband throw the ball, too, but he had to do it *just so*. If, for example, he rolled it too close to the table, where Monkey could possibly bang into one of the legs and hurt herself, I'd scold him. Any misstep with either of the dogs brought out my inner bitch. I'd accuse him of ineptitude, of ruining all my careful work with the dogs, of being careless and clueless. Many times he tried to clean the deepees with a paper towel instead of the flea comb. This spread them instead of removing them, which let my cruel tongue flap to new heights. Of course, it wasn't really about the dogs. Over the years, he'd made me feel like a second class citizen, one who didn't even merit the attention he gave to old newspapers, so now I could let my silent anger break out. While I wasn't as adept as Krista in the show ring, or as smooth an "about turner" as some of those Obedience types, I was competent, and the dogs saw me as alpha. This was something my husband couldn't deride or dismiss. It was something I could do well and he couldn't. Yet, throughout all my tirades, he never told me to shut up. His face might've tightened, his eyes might've narrowed, but his mouth remained closed. He was, I concluded, emotionally constipated.

After Staten Island, there were a couple of trials in upstate New York. I decided to enter Monkey in both of them. One was at Shawangunk and the other at Chenango. It's a good thing I kept a log of these trials. I never could have remembered those names. Argo had returned from a disappointing trip to northern Virginia and Maryland where, in three shows, he garnered no points. For a fleeting moment, I thought, perhaps Krista was losing her touch, but I shoved that idea aside. If she couldn't put points on Argo, who could? Me? I laughed at the absurdity of that notion.

In June, Argo was entered in six shows over two weekends. Krista's magic touch had returned, and he won the points at all of them. At the Burlington County Kennel Club, on June 15, 1997, he became a champion, or more precisely, a champion of record. As I learned the hard way with Mercury, the points had to be confirmed by the AKC before the championship became final. Since Argo was already entered in the sixth show, Shawangunk, Krista handled him, and he won, although he didn't need the point. It was ironic. Mercury couldn't go to Westminster because he was one point short by the deadline date, and here Argo earned an extra point, well in advance of the deadline.

While Argo was winning the point he didn't need, Monkey was busy, too. She was heeling with her focus on me, for a change, not on the bystanders. She must've done a passable job on the other exercises as well. I can't recall the details of her performance, but my notes say that the judge was elderly and lenient. We came in third with a qualifying score of 191.5. With one leg down and two to go, Monkey was on her way to becoming a *bona fide* companion dog.

Later that month, I took her to the Chenango Valley Kennel Club. I was thrilled that Monkey had earned a leg, and I felt confident that she'd get another. But the Novice A judge was dour and strict. I don't know exactly where we went wrong, but Monkey didn't qualify. She didn't qualify at Riverhead the following month, either. The show was indoors and it was noisy and hot. Monkey showed no interest in heeling or in the long sit. I knew what she was thinking, "Why sit if you can lie down and relax?"

I decided to give Monkey the rest of the summer off. What was the point in trekking to Obedience trials when I could sail my boat or take a cooling swim in the bay at Shelter Island? We'd settled in for the summer, and that's where I decided we'd stay. Besides we now had an unofficial champion in the family, which meant it was time to figure out how to get into Westminster.

Chapter 12

Westminster or Bust

I had always planned to show Argo myself. That was my tribute to Mercury. I figured if I could get around the ring without tripping or looking too inept, I'd be happy, and our mission would be complete. After Argo became a champion, I told Krista I was going to handle him. She wasn't disappointed. She had her own Schipperkes preparing for the Garden. I soon discovered that things had changed in the few years since I'd entered Mercury. Now entries were faxed, not mailed. As I asked around, querying the dog people I knew, one name kept popping up: Marge at Blue Ribbon. I learned she was a "faxing agent," a person hired to submit batches of entries from Westminster hopefuls. I loved the sound of "Blue Ribbon." It smacked of prizes and placements and glory. Though I didn't expect to achieve any of these, I called Marge and she agreed to handle my entry.

Summer ended and we returned to the city. I'd entered Monkey in an Obedience trial right after Labor Day in Tuxedo Park. My notes indicate she did well, earning her second leg with a score of 173. My notes also show that the judge was *very* lenient. I'd also brought Argo along. I had entered him as a Special, figuring time with him in the ring would improve our performance at Westminster. Unfortunately, Krista was there, and her Special went Best of Breed.

Monkey and I traveled into the heartland of New Jersey for our next trial. The highway system in this state always befuddled me. Lanes disappeared right out from under the car and exits veered off to the left or right with little predictability. For me, a New Yorker, used to driving the linear routes of the Long Island Expressway and the New York

State Thruway, not to mention the sanely laid out streets of Manhattan, navigating New Jersey's roads was enough to put me back on Prozac. Towards the end of the summer, I had decided to stop taking it. With Westminster coming up, I wanted to re-enter the world of emotion and feeling. I wanted to sense the excitement of preparing for that show, and feel the nervousness that might grab me on our big day in the ring. My involvement, or maybe it was my obsession, with the dogs seemed to have shooed depression away. I even softened my attitude towards my husband.

Somerset looked as if Monkey might triumph. There were no Rottweilers, and the other competitors came from slew of notoriously stubborn breeds, PBGV (Petit Basset Griffon Vendeen) and Sharpei among them. But then I learned that this particular judge was extremely strict. Any dog lagging as much as a centimeter in heeling, lost points. This judge expected perfection, even at Novice A. Of course, Monkey didn't qualify.

The following weekend, I took both dogs to Hatboro, Pennsylvania. At least, that's where we were entered. But thanks to New Jersey's roads, and lack of informative signage, I missed the exit for the Pennsylvania Turnpike and somehow ended up near Philadelphia. I'd left extra time, as usual, but even my zooming at 90 miles per hour to backtrack didn't get us there for Argo's class. That was money down the good old drain, plus a lost opportunity to practice for Westminster. Disgusted, I took the crates out of the car and set up in the shade near the Obedience ring. It was a warm day, and Novice A didn't take place until late in the morning. Monk grew bored, and when we entered the ring, she showed it. My notes reveal that her heeling off leash "was terrible."

The very next day, Portchester held its annual Obedience Trials, and since their focus was on the various levels of performance training, Argo stayed home. Monkey surprised me and did a workmanlike job on all the exercises. How sweet it would be to get that third leg from the place where we'd trained, I thought. During the long sit, I held my breath, and happily, Monk held her position. We were there, I mused, we were *there*. Kebrill's Mothersday Miracle, CD. What a lovely phrase. Next came the three minute Down. I counted silently to myself, but as the second minute began, Monkey made her move. Slowly, as if she figured no one would notice, she slithered across the ring, like a furry black snake, crouched low, advancing on tiny steps through the grass. People laughed. I glared at her. And the judge told me we didn't qualify.

This was our eleventh trial, and each time, Monkey frustrated me by blowing off a different part of the required exercises. I could never foresee what her devious Schipperke mind had in store for me. But I was not going to give up. I had her entered in Queensboro and Bronx County, a Friday through Sunday series that took place in Flushing Meadow, near the site of the old Word's Fair. These were All Breed and Obedience shows, but I left Argo home. My time belonged to Monkey.

At Friday's trial, she surprised me again by messing up the recall, something she'd done almost perfectly at every other event. For this off-lead exercise, she first had to sit and she did. Then I left her and crossed the ring. I stood facing her. The steward signaled me to call her. "Monkey, come!" I said in a loud, cheery voice. But Monk sat there as if to say, "Why don't *you* come to *me*? I called her again and she moseyed towards me, forgetting to sit in front of me before finishing in heel position. In the long Down, the Portuguese Water Dog next to her got up. Monkey thought that was a good idea so she stood as well. These errors, along with her usual sloppy heeling off lead earned us another NQ.

Nasty weather greeted us the next morning. It was rainy and cold under a wintry gray sky. This was trial number thirteen for Miss Monkey, and that number, along with the weather, signalled bad luck. Perhaps Monkey sensed my discouragement, and, to buoy my spirits, performed flawlessly, until the one minute Sit. She was flanked by a Rottweiler and another large dog. This dog, I learned from its proud owner, had earned its CD the day before, and was competing in the trial just for fun, and because the owner had already paid. The dog decided to lie down during the long sit. Monkey followed suit. My heart sank. I wondered how many more of these wretched trials we'd have to attend before she finally earned her title. But a miracle occurred. When the judge announced the scores, Monkey qualified. Her score was 187. Clearly the judge hadn't seen her go down on the long Sit. The Rottweiler had blocked her from his view. I didn't say anything. I accepted the ribbon, we took a photo. I now had a Companion Dog.

I don't know why we bothered with the trial on Sunday. It was a small group, and when Monkey lay down on the Sit, there was no Rottweiler to shield her. She didn't stand for examination either. It was clear she was bored. I was relieved that she had "earned" her title the day before. As soon as we left the ring, Monkey showed me she wanted to go home. She strained at the leash, tugging me in the direction of the parking lot. But unfortunately for her, I had noticed, that in the afternoon, the American Kennel Club was offering Canine Good Citizen tests. I figured, since we already were there, Monkey might as well try it. For this title, a dog had to show good behavior in a variety of situations. It couldn't for example, lunge or growl at a person who came up to shake its owner's hand. It had to walk on a leash without yanking its owner off his or her feet. And it couldn't freak out when an umbrella suddenly was opened nearby. Plus it had to be nice to children. This part worried me because kids found Monkey so adorable, that on the street they'd rush over, squealing, hovering over her, trying to pet her. Often she'd back away. She never growled or showed teeth. She just wasn't particularly fond of children. Yet, when the tykes who were part of this test entered the ring and approached her, she stood still and let them touch her. I was so proud of my Monkey. In addition to a companion dog, she was now a canine good citizen.

None of these titles changed Monkey's personality. She still went berserk when she saw the Chihuahuas, and in the park, she might heel for a few steps before rushing out to the end of her Flexilead.® This became a game for her. I'd repeat the command, and she'd return to heel position, then look up at me for a moment as if to say, "See, I can do this but it's more fun to be out in front." And off she'd go. Argo always surged ahead, but I didn't correct him. A show dog needs animation and fluid movement and should never lag at the handler's side. That's why dog people warn newcomers not to Obedience train their show dogs. Argo was as frisky as a young colt. I never worried about him hanging back.

My husband was thrilled with Monkey's achievement, even though I confessed that a Rottweiler had helped her succeed. To my mind, it didn't matter. I knew she knew the exercises. She'd shown she could do them. She just chose not to do all of them correctly on the same day. That's what made Monkey, Monkey. She had a mind of her own.

Shortly after these trials, I received the printout of the shows Argo had competed in, detailing the points he'd won at each event. I'd never had any doubts that he had the right amount to get into Westminster, and that he'd earned them by the proper deadline. Now it was a question of waiting for the crate pass to arrive in the mail, hoping that Marge at Blue Ribbon had been successful. I started musing about the Garden and what it was going to be like. One of the things I realized right off was that I needed the proper outfit. No long flowering skirts with sequined tops for this gig, even though such fashion *faux pas* frequently cropped up at the Garden for Best in Show. By asking around, I discovered that blue was the color judges favored for women that year. On the other hand, men often caught the judge's eye by wearing a dark green jacket. So now, I had a fashion mission. The hunt for a suit began. Unfortunately for me, royal blue suits were as common in New York stores in the fall as yellow submarines were in the U.S. navy at any time of year. The suit had to have pockets, preferably in the skirt, so I could easily insert my hand and pull out a tasty liver treat to keep Argo interested in following me around the ring. I decided to take a tour of Manhattan's Upper East Side thrift shops. These stores, benefitting charities such as cancer care and child adoptions, received the cast offs of New York socialites. Maybe blue was last year's color and I'd hit one of the stores just after one of these women had cleaned out her closet to make way for this year's trends. Most of the women wore small sizes, as did I, and their clothes came from designers. Some items had been worn once, maybe twice. This appealed to me, especially since the prices were affordable if I found the right outfit. Instead of paying $1500, I might get by with $250. I can't recall which thrift shop had the gem I ended up buying, but I do recall seeing a swath of royal blue in the rack, and gently pulling on it. Was it just a jacket or a complete suit? My heartbeat increased as I pushed aside the adjacent clothes to reveal my find. It *was* a suit, an Armani, and the size on the tag read 38. Perfect. I took it into the fitting room. Both the skirt and the jacket had pockets and I pictured myself striding around the ring, smartly attired, my champion trotting with verve at the end of his show lead. On my feet, I'd wear the pair of Belgian shoes I'd used in earlier shows. These were flat slip-ons with tiny leather bows, where, on traditional loafers, a penny would've been tucked. They were super comfortable, and I'd had them customized with treaded rubber half soles. This gave me just enough traction to glide around the ring without slipping. I should probably add that I paid full price for these beauties. They fit my feet like a glove, and the leather was as smooth and supple as a puppy's belly.

Right after Thanksgiving, I reviewed our position. I had my shoes, I had my suit, and Argo had his championship. Now it was a question of waiting to see if we were in. There was no point in calling Marge. She handled so many entries, it would have been impossible for her to know the status of each. I had no choice but to go on with life and hope that one day soon a crate pass and judging program would show up in my mailbox.

Chapter 13

Argo's Big Day

One morning, I was struggling to iron the wrinkles out of a couple of silk nightgowns I'd hand washed. "Struggle" was the right word because, as with vacuum cleaners, I always managed to get caught up in the electrical cords. That's why we sent most of our stuff out to the laundry, and we had someone come in to handle the cleaning. But on this particular morning, staying home to iron proved fateful. The phone rang. I picked it up. A voice asked for me, stumbling over my name. Aha, I thought, a telemarketer. I was just about to hang up, accusing the caller of being a nuisance when she said, "I'm an editor." An *editor*. Whoa. I quickly put a cheery smile into my voice and apologized for my snippiness. We chatted, and I eagerly accepted the assignment she offered of writing a dog book for the Barron's Educational Series. The editor said she had read a few articles I'd written about Schipperkes. I didn't ask which ones, in case she'd mistaken me for someone else. I hadn't exactly flooded the print world with work on the subject of dogs. In fact, I could only recall two pieces I'd done, and they had appeared in the DWAA (Dog Writers' Association of America) newsletter, which had a limited circulation. In any event, writing *Schipperkes. A Complete Pet Owner's Manual* would keep me busy throughout the coming year. I'd talk to breeders and do research, learning more and more about these little black devils along the way. I decided that any money I made from book sales would go right to Schipperke Rescue.

I sensed that Bruce was impressed, though he couldn't find the words to say so out loud. Yet he did manage to express emotion a week or so later. The crate pass and judging program arrived. We were *in*. My husband said something like, "That's terrific," but he didn't slap me on the back or let out a whoop of joy. Then he said he'd call a business acquaintance who had a sky box at the Garden and see if we could have access to it the day Argo was shown. I could tell he was thrilled. His "son" was going to the 122nd annual Westminster Kennel Club Dog Show. The next day, in the park, I told everyone the big news.

I was happy to have the book project to help fill the weeks before February 16th, the first day of the two-day show, and the day on which the non-sporting breeds were shown. This group was a *bouillabaisse* of breeds and included, among others, American Eskimo Dogs, Bulldogs, Chinese Shar-Pei, Chow Chows, Dalmations, Miniature and Standard Poodles, Tibetan Spaniels and Schipperkes. These were breeds that no longer were used for their original purposes, i.e. Poodles as hunting dogs. Lucky for Argo, he would only have to compete against other Schipperkes. He was a handsome dog, but there was no way he would go Best of Breed and move up to the next level of competition, Group. There were too many big name Schipperkes entered. Besides, he had me as his handler. Blue suit notwithstanding, I knew I couldn't outshine the owner/breeder/handlers who'd been to hundreds of shows and whose lives revolved around dogs.

The moment Bruce received the o.k. on the sky box, I invited a bunch of friends to the show. The boxes were situated just under the roof of the Garden, and each had its own big screen TV, plus endless refreshments. A special elevator, guarded by a square jawed fellow with a buzz cut, led to the carpeted corridors that gave access to the various suites. Looking down at the rings from this height, the dogs resembled prancing ants. I, of course, had to stay in the benching area with Argo. Benched shows used to be popular way back, but nowadays, I believe, only Philadelphia and Westminster are organized this way. Each exhibitor receives a crate pass which corresponds to a numbered spot on a "bench", which really resembles an elongated shelf set a few inches off the floor. The rows are arranged by breeds and crate size so that small breeds find themselves at one end of the benching area, followed by breeds that fit into medium sized crates, followed by the large breeds. From 11:00 a.m. until shortly before 8:00 p.m. when everyone heads towards the exit, the dogs must be in their crates on the bench. An AKC official might stop by for a check, and issue the absentee a warning. No exhibitor wants that. Naturally, time is allowed for showing in the ring and for potty breaks, which take place indoors, in specially erected, sawdust-covered canine comfort stations.

The show that year fell on President's Day weekend, which meant record crowds and lots of kids who had the day off from school. Anyone who has ever attended this dog show certainly remembers how packed the aisles became and how slowly people moved as they tried to get around. I figured it was going to be extra hot and stuffy that Monday, Argo's day in the show ring. That's why I bought a crate fan. This battery-run gadget affixed to the door and helped circulate the air. Of course, a handler could take a dog out of its crate so people could pet and admire it, but Argo wasn't that gregarious. I knew he'd rather sack out on his faux leopard mat, under the whir of the fan.

As the Big Day approached, I wanted to have everything run smoothly. Though we lived about two miles from the Garden, on the route of the Number 4 bus that could deposit us a short block from the entrance, I opted for private transportation. I reserved the Pet Taxi. For a price way higher than public transportation, and a premium over a normal taxi fare, this service sent a small mini-van with plenty of room for a dog, a crate, a bag of grooming tools, an anxious husband and me. I can't recall what we paid, but it was worth not having to stand in the street, trying to find a cab that would take two humans, a dog and a batch of gear.

I had bought a dolly especially for this event so Argo could roll into the Garden in his wire crate. As I imagined our entrance, the triumphal march from *Aida* swirled through my head. But things turned out quite differently. Oh, yes, the Pet Taxi arrived on time at 7:30 in the morning. I had the doorman take a picture of my husband, Argo and me standing in front of the bright yellow vehicle. Then off we went to the Garden. I alone could enter through the Exhibitors gate, so I said "bye bye" to my husband and sent him up to the sky box. I loaded Argo's crate onto the dolly and we rolled into the staging area. At the bottom of a ramp, exhibitors and their dogs were boarding a huge freight elevator, the kind that could fit two elephants, a hippo, and a half dozen horses, but not Argo and me. The gates closed before us, and we had to wait several minutes for the car to return. We had plenty of time. Schipperkes didn't go to the ring until 11:00.

"Zoo" best described the scene as we exited the elevator. Throngs of exhibitors pressed forward like crazed youths at a rock concert, toting their dogs and paraphernalia, pushing, but not quite shoving, their way towards the benching area. Someone made a snide remark about my dolly taking up too much room, but I ignored it. This was my day, and Argo's, and, of course, Mercury's. No one was going to spoil it. On the way in, some exhibitors stopped at the section set aside for grooming, to put up their tables. This was a spot where spectators could observe a Standard Poodle getting its three-hour "hairdo," or watch a groomer adjust the coils on a Komondor. Luckily, Schipperkes didn't require such fussing. A good spray with a water bottle, then a brushing, and a Schip was ready to show. This grooming was easily done with the dog perched atop its crate in the benching area.

I wheeled Argo over to the row where Schipperkes were benched and found our slot, number 18, which was also our catalog number. I tucked the dolly into the small space below, placed the crate on the bench, put water in the small dish that attached to the door, and set up the fan. My boy now had all the comforts of home, except that he was confined. Yet he never complained. He wasn't a yappy dog. He was royalty, a descendant of Mercury, Prince of Dogs. Soon other Schipperke people arrived and set up. I knew Krista had two of her Schips entered, but she also handled other breeds, so I figured, correctly, that she'd set up in the section for handlers with multiple entries. This was just as well. Seeing her would only remind me of my lack of skill in the ring.

I'd brought a small padlock and secured it to Argo's crate, just in case any dognappers might roam the aisles. There was plenty of time before the official benching began, which was the exact time we had to head to the ring. I made my way to the sky box. My friends had arrived and were enjoying coffee and croissants. A huge platter of fruit and a selection of cheeses were on the sideboard, as well as bottles of wine. It was early in the day so no one was interested in alcohol, except Bruce. He was drinking a beer. He also was chatting and making people laugh. This was a side of him I rarely saw. It seemed he had another personality, one he kept hidden for special occasions and for the amusement of others, not me. I grabbed a few grapes and a bottle of water. I told everyone I'd stop up later, after Argo's turn in the ring. They wished me good luck, and off I went, embarking on the greatest doggie adventure of my life.

There were twenty-one Schipperkes entered that year, the largest number ever. I took Argo out of his crate. Then I slipped on his show lead, sprayed and brushed him, ran my hands over his nuts to alert him to what was coming, popped some liver treats into my pocket, and headed towards the ring. We lined up on the side, waiting for the Standard Poodles to leave. I'd brought the water bottle and brush for last minute touch ups, and then the steward called our class. Except for the Specialty, I'd never seen so many Schipperkes in one place. I wasn't sure where to stand. The steward had called for catalog order, but it seemed everyone was milling around, as if out for a play date in the park. Then the steward separated dogs and bitches. Luckily, another exhibitor told me what was happening so I didn't end up showing Argo with the bitches. The table exam would have unmasked him anyway, and humiliated me. Despite not knowing what was what, I wasn't nervous.

I felt as though I were in a surreal drama. Physically, I was in the ring, but at the same time, I wasn't. I was *watching* and *being* simultaneously. When it was our turn, I took Argo around the ring and put him on the table for examination. So far, so good, I thought. I hadn't tripped, and Argo hadn't shied away from the judge. We returned to our place and waited for the remaining Schipperkes to be judged. People who show a lot recognize the hand and arm signals that a judge gives which tell exhibitors when to move, when to stop, and when to leave the ring. I kept an eye on the people around me because I still wasn't sure what to do. I noticed Krista on the sidelines along with another handler I knew as a "face." So when the judge motioned for the group I was in to go around again, I figured it was the *sayonara* circle. He'd thank us and we'd all leave the ring. But instead he raised his hand, and flicking his fingers, as if dispensing holy water, he signaled one, two, three, four, five. A whoop and a shriek went up from the bystanders. The "one" and "two" were suddenly crushed by kissing well-wishers. I stood there, completely at sea, not understanding that Argo and I had just won a coveted Award of Merit. This award is given to dogs who, in the judge's opinion, are outstanding representatives of their breed, but not as fine as the ones selected Best of Breed and Best of Opposite. Three Awards of Merit were handed out in Schipperkes that day, and Argo came in second. One of Krista's entries, which she hadn't handled, won the first AOM. When Mr. Bernfeld, the judge, handed me our ribbon and Award, I thanked him. He was the same judge who gave Mercury Best of Breed at Brookhaven, the start of our Westminster entry problems, and here he was bestowing this incredible canine honor on Argo. Champion Kebrill's Mercurial Argonaut had closed the circle at last. He'd brought home "the golden fleece" in a bigger way than I ever could have imagined.

When it came time to have our photo taken, Argo had had enough. He refused to stand on the table and sat. John Ashby, the well-known dog show photographer, tried to get Argo's attention by throwing rubber toys and making funny noises. But he didn't have all day, and he couldn't influence Argo. Nor could I. Finally Mr. Ashby told me to let him sit. This was known as an informal pose, and I'm willing to bet, it's the only one ever taken at Westminster with a dog sitting.

I brought Argo back to his crate. I couldn't wait to go up to the sky box and show everyone the purple and gold ribbon and the Award of Merit. The handsome round medallion came in a velvet lined presentation box. On one side, in relief, stood the Pointer, and, circling the edge, the words Westminster Kennel Club. On the back, again in relief, it read Award of Merit. The year, 1998, was engraved below that. One of my friends had a video camera with sound and "interviewed" me as I held up the medal and the ribbon. If I hadn't had to go back to the benching area and hang around until almost 8 p.m., I would've drunk a glass of Champagne.

Argo dozed in his crate and I chatted with people who came by. I could tell them a lot about Schipperkes, their history, their personalities and their care. I was, thanks to the book project, becoming somewhat of an expert.

As I had predicted, it was especially crowded, hot and stuffy that Monday. I'd long since taken off my jacket, and the silk blouse I'd worn under it was soaked through at the armpits. I was glad the batteries propelling Argo's fan hadn't run out of juice. Somehow the afternoon and early evening hours passed. They were anti-climactic, of course. Shortly before 8:00, everyone, except those dogs who'd gone Best of Breed and now had to compete in their respective groups, headed towards the freight elevator and the exit. Outside, on the street, I found a regular taxi. I loaded Argo's crate and dolly into the trunk, put him on my lap, and we headed home. Monkey greeted us at the door, just ahead of my husband who had opened a bottle of Pommery. It was 9 p.m. and I was pooped. I drank Champagne, had a light supper and went to bed. I didn't have to dream about Westminster. It had already come true.

Chapter 14

Life After Westminster

What was Argo's reward for his Westminster triumph? A mating with a seductive bitch in season? A basketful of juicy bones? A trip to the dog biscuit factory? Unfortunately for him, none of these. We decided to have him snipped, or neutered. I had no interest in offering his services as a stud dog. Argo had a wide open pedigree, which meant he had a lot of different bloodlines in his make-up. Most breeders choose, and then breed for, a specific type. Argo had too much variety in his genes to make him a desirable suitor. I also didn't want to bring more Schipperkes into this world. That job was for serious breeders, not an amateur like me. Neutering, I hoped, would also curb his sex drive. Though I never allowed him to hump people's legs, sometimes he'd start before I could prevent it. As soon as I saw this, I'd pull him off. Already "in gear," he'd go bucking around the living room, humping the air, as if he had a willing female in his clutches. Observers laughed, but I felt sorry for him. Clearly this was a dog that needed a girlfriend, a little furry-butted bitch that would tease him and please him. I tried to ease his frustration. This was a secret that only Bruce knew, though I didn't tell him outright. He read about it. I'd written an essay in the *The New York Press* about Argo's amorous needs. It was published under a pseudonym because of its descriptively raunchy and detailed content, but my husband figured it out. The editor had called our home phone while I was away visiting my friend Dorothy in Virginia. Because of the upcoming deadline, Bruce had given the editor the number where I could be reached. Though I won't elaborate, as I did in that newspaper piece, readers who don't want to know any more about this subject should skip to the next paragraph, now. I knew Argo needed sexual release, so I helped him. Sleeve up, I'd let him straddle my arm and rub against it, until he ejaculated. I never thought, "yuk," or "eeeww." This was clean, untainted stuff from inside my dog, and it washed off in a jiffy. My champion Argo. He'd whimper at climax, just like a man. In all my research, I must admit, I never asked anyone if they had helped their intact males get relief in this way. But I suspected they did.

Like Mercury, Argo and Monkey loved to travel. Bruce and I continued our annual winter trips with them to Puerto Rico, to the same resort where we'd taken Mercury. As soon as I placed the Sherpa® bags in the living room, these Schipperkes climbed inside and lay there. Monkey's expression seemed to say, "Hurry up. Let's get this show on the road."

On one of these trips, on the way home, our flight was delayed four hours. We sat in the terminal, waiting. There was no place to walk the dogs since we no longer were allowed outside. Happily, they didn't embarrass us. In fact, they were better behaved than most of the human travelers. When we finally boarded, we languished on the tarmac for another hour. It was hot in the cabin. Kids were crying. I took Argo out of his bag and sprayed him with cold water, using the bottle I always kept for these emergencies. Bruce, in the row behind me, already had Monkey on his lap. We gave them each a biscuit. Both dogs never made a sound, and when we finally took off, they went back into their bags and slept until we landed in New York.

In Puerto Rico, the two of them loved to run on the beach. Back then, this resort had no leash laws. Some people had condos there and came down for a few weeks or months each winter, bringing their dogs with them. I remember Jeremy, the Basset Hound, and Georgie Girl, a PBGV, who was also a champion show dog, and who had met Mercury a few years back. Argo and Monkey looked forward to seeing their canine pals and learning Spanish. I taught them to respond to, "*Sientense, perros,*" which made everyone chuckle as the two Schips sat on command.

My husband, whose fair skin couldn't take the sun, stayed indoors in the air conditioning, except for morning forays to the tennis courts, followed by a quick swim in the ocean. The villa we rented had an upstairs and downstairs, two bedrooms, two baths and a patio. It was big enough for a real family, and for a dog family, it was a palace. Monkey and Argo loved to dart up and down the stairs, zigzagging across the marble floor like furry quarterbacks. We made one last trip to Puerto Rico after 9/11, and that time we paid for the dogs' round-trip tickets. We probably could have sneaked them on as we'd been doing for years, but now it didn't feel right. Besides, as the author of a respected book on Schipperkes, I couldn't risk getting caught and perhaps having a story appear in the tabloids or on Fox News.

When we returned to the city, I decided to put another title on Monkey: Novice Agility Dog, or NAD. After she received her CD, I had started her on Agility training at Portchester. The variety of obstacles intrigued her. She especially enjoyed those that had targets, such as the A-frame. These paper plate targets always contained a treat, and the idea was for the dog to run the entire obstacle and touch down in the right place, on target. When the dog understood what was required, the targets were removed. This worked in most cases. But Monkey kept searching for the treat, squeezing under the obstacle and vacuuming the floor for crumbs. It was a challenge to train her out of this, and I finally told the instructor to remove the targets. Clicker training was gaining popularity at the time, and a few of the handlers in our class began using them. These were noisy gadgets and Monkey hated the sound. She'd start panting, her tongue hanging out, and then bolt towards the exit, ignoring my command to come. Luckily the door always was closed.

After she'd learned all the obstacles, and could run a course, I entered her in some trials. I didn't know it at the time, but this was going to be a repeat of our Obedience odyssey. Monkey would always find one obstacle to exit or run around. She especially disliked the seesaw. On this obstacle, a dog had to walk up one side, pause and shift its weight slightly, so it could come down on the other side as the "see" "sawed." I didn't keep a log of her Agility trials, but I do remember we went to a lot of them. I was getting tired of driving out to the countryside, to far off farms and fields, the only locations where there was enough land to set up the courses. Monk earned her first two legs in typical Monkey fashion—running a perfect round one day, then hopping off the A-frame or Dog Walk the next. I do remember the day she got her NAD. We'd had a clear round and were headed towards the dreaded seesaw. I watched Monkey walk up, then pause and look down at the ground, measuring the distance as a prelude to jumping off. I said to her, out of the corner of my mouth, "Don't you dare." Our eyes met, and she knew I was serious. She tipped the seesaw down and exited it perfectly. Then someone in the background clicked a clicker. Monk took off for the parking lot before I could get her on the leash. Luckily, when she realized she was in unknown territory, she responded when I yelled, in my fed up voice, "Monkey. Come!"

The Schipperke National Specialty was in Carlisle, Pennsylvania that spring, a drivable distance from the city. I thought it would be fun to meet other Schipperke people and waltz Monkey and Argo across the auditorium in the Parade of Titleholders. I also was interested in meeting the Famous Clicker Trainer (FCT) who was giving a seminar. I won't reveal her name, because Monkey embarrassed her in front of lots of people, but I'll give a clue that she'd written a well-received book on clicker training and had been a guest on a doggy television show. The morning of the seminar, I watched as she conditioned a 6 month old puppy with this training technique. The idea was to click, then give a treat when the dog responded to a command. Gradually, treats were withdrawn, and only the clicker was used. Monkey saw through this right away. Why would she obey a sound? She wanted the treat. The FCT announced that any dog could be trained using the clicker. She was willing to demonstrate this with a volunteer. I raised my hand. "My dog hates the clicker," I said. "It makes her crazy."

People gathered round. The FCT approached Monkey. She petted her and spoke softly to her. Monk accepted this and even seemed interested in the woman, probably because she smelled of food. In one hand, the FCT held a piece of steak, and in the other, the clicker. She showed Monk the steak and told her to sit. That's when Monk saw the clicker. She turned her head away from the steak and took a step backwards. The FCT waved the steak under Monkey's nose, but Monkey knew it was a trap. Again she refused. She crawled under my chair. The FCT relented. "I've never seen a dog turn down steak," she said.

"You've never met a dog like Miss Monkey," I replied.

Bruce thought I should pack it in and just enjoy the dogs as pets, the way he did. But I had bigger dreams. Now that Monkey had two titles, it was Argo's turn. I decided to train him in Obedience. To make traveling easier, I brought my car back to the city. Argo weighed about five pounds more than Monkey. Carrying him on and off the bus in his bag, en route to the Metro North station, was like hauling a sack of potatoes. Argo enjoyed the car ride, but when it came to dog school, he was a dunce. It's not that he didn't understand the exercises, he just couldn't see the point in doing them. Although the instructor encouraged us to use treats during training, I didn't want to keep popping them into his mouth. Unlike the big dogs, who could down a bagful of jerky at every class with no side effects, Argo would suffer from goody overload, which often resulted in dirty poopies.

After weeks of classes and practice at home, I entered him in a trial. I had to sign up for Novice B, which put more pressure on me. Unlike Novice A, "B" was for handlers who'd already put an Obedience title on a dog. A certain level of competence was expected, and although I had improved since my forays with Monkey, I still wasn't smooth like the handlers who lived and loved Obedience.

I kept a list, but not a detailed log, of Argo's Obedience adventures. It surprises me to this day, when I look at my notebook, that he qualified at that first trial. He had a "squeak by" score of 171.5. Unfortunately, it was downhill after that. Ten trials later, he still hadn't earned another leg. At one indoor event, which I can still picture, he stopped in the middle of the ring on the off lead heeling. Somewhere, on the other side of the building, there was a hot dog vendor. Argo picked up the scent. Nose twitching in the air, he trotted towards the exit. "Why am I doing these dumb exercises when there's food to be had," he probably thought. Luckily a steward caught him and grabbed his collar.

Finally, on our eleventh attempt, Argo got another leg. This was at Queensboro, which made it all the more satisfying since this was the trial where Monkey had received her CD two years earlier. It also took place on October 29th, Mercury's birthday. I viewed these two coincidences as a sign that Argo was on his way to his title. I should've known better. He was, first and foremost, a Schipperke. He had already formed his mind set for the things that motivated him. They were, in this order: treats, treats and more treats. Some breeds thrive on praise. Schipperkes demand the pay off.

I took him to eight more trials, but there was always a glitch in our performance. Often, it was my fault. I'd give a command twice if he didn't respond, and this took points off. Other times, it was his bored attitude that did us in. I recall a trial where I told him to heel and he sat in place as I moved off. I saw the judge smiling. I looked back to see Argo rolling over onto his back as if he expected someone to step forward and scratch his belly. At Staten Island, where I'd pulled Monkey out of the melee of growling, scuffling dogs, I also retired Argo. For sits and downs, he was positioned next to a male Rottweiler. I couldn't take the chance. He'd already raised his scruff at this dog when we lined up to wait our respective turns to enter the ring. I asked the judge if she would move us next to smaller dogs. She said no. I told her I wasn't going to risk my dog's life and that I was withdrawing. She said she understood, and for official purposes said, "O.k., your dog is sick. You're excused."

Argo wasn't having fun and neither was I. So I told him, that was it, we were quitting. Though normally I finish whatever I start, in this case, I made an exception. Both Argo and Monkey were now free to enjoy their lives as house pets.

Chapter 15

Eva

One Friday, in the spring of 2000, we were getting ready to go to Shelter Island for the weekend. I had just finished putting the Schips and their crates into the car, when out of the corner of my eye, I saw a big white dog. It was running in our direction, on a leash, pulling a small woman who was trying to slow it without success. As the pair arrived in front of our building, the woman called out, "Can you help me?"

I clapped my hands and drew the dog's attention. The woman, out of breath, shortened the leash and thanked me. The dog stood between us, wagging its tail with such vigor, it seemed as if it might fly right off its body. "I need to find a home for this dog," the woman said.

Just then, our doorman came out. The dog jumped on him, stretching to its full height. On its hind legs, its head was level with the man's. The dog licked him, and he laughed. "Maybe you want her," the woman said. The doorman shook his head.

"I found her in the South Bronx, or should I say, she found me," she added. "It's a long story."

"I'm on my way out of town," I said. "Give me your phone number and I'll call you over the weekend. I know a lot of dog people. Maybe I can help you. What's your name?"

"Ana. Ana Pacheco."

"And the dog?"

"Eva."

I signaled for my husband to bring me a pen and the small notebook I kept tucked in the pocket of the driver's side door. I took Ana's information and got into the car. Eva watched, and perhaps smelling the Schipperkes inside, or just wanting to go for a ride, took one big lunge towards the vehicle. Ana yanked her back. My husband, in the front passenger's seat, shot me a look that said, "Let's get going." As I pulled away from the curb, out of the rearview mirror, I saw Ana and Eva turn the corner.

It was unusual to see a Pit Bull Terrier on Fifth Avenue, for that's what Eva was. A block away, in the housing projects, they were the dogs of choice, along with Rottweilers. Seldom did these dogs' owners walk them on or near Fifth Avenue, at least not in the daytime in the year 2000. This wasn't always the case. Before Rudy Giuiliani became mayor, the area of Central Park, across the street from our building and stretching north to its upper boundary at 110th Street, hosted a variety of criminal activities. The Central Park Jogger was brutalized nearby, drug dealers met nightly and the smell of marijuana could make a passerby get high. Then there were the dogs. I'd sometimes see them being "trained," muscular Pit Bulls, hanging off the ground, their jaws firmly clamped on a tire or log, undoubtedly baited with meat, or blood. The fights took place well inside the park, very late at night, and for the most part, free of police intervention. In that tumultuous era, the cops had murders and robberies to deal with. They ignored the cockfights and dogs.

I was curious about Eva, and the "long story" connected with her, so over the weekend, I called Ana. She told me she'd been in the South Bronx, feeding stray cats, something she routinely does, when she saw a skinny white dog roaming loose on the street. In that part of town, homeless and abandoned dogs were a common sight, so Ana continued on her way. But the dog followed her. Ana tried to shoo her off. After all, what could Ana possibly do with a dog? She had a houseful of cats that she'd rescued, living at her home in Manhattan. Ana went into a deli to buy more cat food. When she exited the store, there was the dog, sitting, waiting for her. Ana's heart went out to this scrawny, sad-looking creature. It was as if, Ana told me, the dog realized that Ana was her only hope of escaping a grim life and certain death on the streets. Ana decided to bring the dog home, but now she faced another problem. She lived in Manhattan and this was miles away, in the South Bronx. The dog had no leash, and even if she did, there was no way Ana could take her on a bus or a subway. She was certain no taxi would stop for a Pit Bull.

Luck was on her side that night. A man and his wife had come out of the deli a few minutes earlier and had noticed the dog. When Ana approached the dog, the man asked if it was hers. Ana told him her story. He had a minivan parked right there and offered to drive them home. With no urging, Eva hopped right in. On the way, they stopped at a pet store and Ana bought a collar and leash. Once home, Ana set up a place for Eva in her basement. There were thirteen cats roaming around upstairs. It didn't seem like a good idea to let the dog see them.

Even Ana, a cat lady, recognized that Eva was a mess. Her nipples drooped, indicating she recently had had puppies and her coat was filthy. She probably had worms. Ana surmised that the male puppies had been taken to train as fighters, and the females as brood bitches, or bait. Eva was lucky. She avoided that dreadful fate by being left to fend for herself. Ana brought her to the Animal Medical Center where, thanks to their state-of-the-art facilities, Eva was returned to health. She received all her shots, got spayed, and now was ready to find a good home. But first she needed training.

She was a young dog and full of energy. The veterinarian had estimated her age at about a year and a half. I told Ana that I would train Eva at no charge. After all, I had experience in Obedience. I didn't mention how many trials it took me with Monkey, or that I'd quit with Argo. It didn't matter. I now had a new challenge. Ana lived on East 101st Street, on the other side of Park Avenue, just past the projects. She owned a rowhouse on a tree-lined block in a neighborhood that was "emerging." It was in Spanish Harlem, and at night, drugs still were sold in the area. But her house and those adjacent to it were lovely. They dated from 1896 and were built in the Renaissance style. Stone steps led to the front door, and another door, set back from the street behind a short iron fence, led to the basement. That's where Ana had set up a bed and a desk so she could stay with Eva. I soon realized that in addition to the dog, I'd have to train Ana. She spoke to Eva like a child. Meanwhile the dog jumped all over her, practically knocking her down. I told Ana to raise her knee when Eva tried to jump on her and say, "Off." Then she was to praise Eva. I explained that she shouldn't play tug of war with Eva because she always lost, and the dog didn't see her as alpha. Each of these suggestions sparked an argument. Used to cats all her life, Ana was having trouble understanding that dogs were different.

I had bought a choke chain, which Ana thought was a cruel device, but I explained, that used properly, it would help keep Eva under control on walks. I reminded Ana of the way I first met her, being dragged down Fifth Avenue by Eva. She finally agreed to use it. Eva learned quickly. Sit. Down. Off. After a few weeks of daily training, she understood what I wanted, although she was better at "sit" and "down" than "off." She loved people, and couldn't contain the urge to jump up and lick their faces. My husband fell in love with her. But as he did with the Schipperkes, he negated my hard work. He let Eva jump all over him and kiss him. This annoyed me. Now I had two humans and a dog to train.

I took Eva for walks in Central Park after I walked the Schips. Ana and I had made flyers with Eva's picture and I gave them to people who stopped to admire her. I asked if they might want to adopt her or if they knew anyone who could. One afternoon, a woman ran up to me in the park and announced that Eva was a Dogo Argentino. She was so excited to see one here, in New York City. The woman herself was from Buenos Aires and she said this was the dog of her country. Later, I looked up Dogos on the Internet, and the animal pictured resembled Eva. I called Ana. If Eva was a Dogo, perhaps we could find her a home through Dogo Rescue.

On a bright Saturday morning, Ana, Eva, Bruce and I set out for Whippany, New Jersey. There, a woman affiliated with Dogo Rescue would tell us whether or not Eva belonged to that breed. I'd asked my husband to drive because Ana was unable to keep Eva in the back seat, where she wouldn't interfere with the person behind the wheel. This way, I could sit in the back and hold onto her. I'd also brought some bully sticks for her to chew.

We drove for miles on the turnpike, then onto secondary roads, then onto even smaller roads that snaked through the countryside. Bruce didn't snarl audibly, but I could tell by the set of his mouth that he was ticked. I can't recall how long it took, but it seemed like hours until we arrived at the address. The moment the woman appeared in the doorway with her own Dogo at her side, I knew we'd wasted the trip. The Dogo stood tall, like a white Great Dane. Compared to him, Eva looked like a dwarf. She's a Pit Bull," I said to Ana, "so let's accept that."

I'd already called a group that rescues and re-homes Pit Bulls, but they told me they had too many dogs at their facility and couldn't take any more. It didn't matter. Ana didn't want to turn Eva over to a shelter, no matter how well-run or caring. She couldn't let Eva go like that, and I had to agree. I promised I'd continue to help her find a forever home for the dog.

My brother-in-law fell in love with Eva, too, and said that he'd take her if he didn't have Casey, his fifteen year-old Westie. My husband and I would adopt her, if we didn't have the Schipperkes. Everyone I talked to had similar stories. Most people who loved dogs, already had a dog or two. I sent flyers to members of the Portchester Obedience and Training Club, hoping that perhaps someone outside the city, with a yard or large property, might be interested. But no one could take her.

Ana was Colombian and she had a fiery Latin temper. Often she'd question me about some aspect of Eva's training or care until I'd lose patience and politely, and sometimes not so politely, tell her to be quiet. Then we'd have an argument. I might say, for example, that Eva should take a monthly pill, prescribed by a veterinarian, to prevent worms. Ana would ask why does she need that, how do you know, who is the veterinarian, I want to call him, how do you know this is safe, what are the ingredients? She was like a magpie on meth.

Every spring, on Shelter Island there is a 10 kilometer foot race followed by a community barbecue. The runners passed in front of our house, and for years, Bruce and I toasted them with Champagne. We were fixtures on the route. I suggested to Ana that I bring Eva to the island that weekend. She could watch the race with us, wearing the "adopt me" t-shirt I'd made from one of my husband's discards, then toodle on over to the barbecue, where maybe, just maybe, we'd find a family looking for a wonderful, sweet tempered dog. On the drive out, Ana began torturing me with questions. This time they were conversation-makers. She asked about my family, then began an inquisition on each one: What does your brother do? Where does he live? How many kids? And on and on it went, until I asked her, loudly, to be quiet or I'd throw her out of the car. I explained I couldn't concentrate on driving. She started mimicking me. I pulled off the highway and stopped the car. I opened the trunk. Then I took out Eva's supplies for the weekend which included her bed and food. Ana had planned to stay overnight at a bed and breakfast, so I tossed her bag out of the car, too. I said, "I've had enough of you. Fend for yourself."

I hopped into the car and slammed the door. But I couldn't leave them there. I drove a few yards and stopped. We reloaded the gear and continued on to Shelter Island, a tense silence between us. The road race and barbecue didn't pan out. Once again, people admired Eva. They petted her and chuckled at her saggy "adopt me" shirt, but not a one even said they might know somebody who was looking for a great companion.

Monkey and Argo had come out with my husband that weekend, arriving late Friday night. They already had met "the big doggie." One afternoon, back in the city, I was walking Eva in the park when she suddenly lunged at a squirrel. She almost pulled me off my feet, and it wasn't until I took her back to Ana's that I realized I didn't have my keys. They must've fallen out of my pocket when Eva jerked me forward. We returned to the park and looked around without finding them. I had no choice but to take her to my apartment and wait until Ana arrived home from work. My doorman had a key to my apartment, so that wasn't a problem. I had told Monkey and Argo all about the "big doggie," especially since they often smelled her on my clothes. Now they would meet her in person, on their home turf. There was no way I could arrange a neutral encounter. I could hear them at the door as I stepped off the elevator. I told them the "big doggie" was here. When I opened the door, the Schips swirled around Eva and chased her down the hallway into the living room. Tail tucked between her legs, she crouched in submission. Then Argo started growling. I sensed he might attack, so I quickly put Eva in the bedroom with a couple of bully sticks and some toys. I called and left a message on Ana's machine. When she came home, hours later, she stopped by and picked up the dog.

I continued working with Eva. She had learned to walk on the leash without pulling, except if she saw a squirrel. One afternoon, Ana joined me for a walk in Central Park. A police scooter was parked near the 102nd Street entrance. Eva was wearing the choke chain which didn't have any identification or her license tag. She went right up to the scooter and stood on her hind legs to say "hi" to the officer inside. Her tongue hung out, ready for a kiss. Ana panicked. "She has tags, she has tags," she said. I whispered for her to be quiet. The officer petted Eva and let her lick him. I asked the officer if he knew anyone who might want to adopt her, but he didn't. Ana and I continued our walk. She had been upset because she thought we might get a ticket for not having a license tag. In her neighborhood, people sometimes were stopped and ticketed for this infraction. I assured her, that here, on Fifth Avenue, there was a different set of rules.

Our efforts to find a home for Eva by showing her off locally hadn't worked, so we expanded our campaign. On the Internet, we found the names of veterinarians, animal shelters, and rescue groups in New Jersey, New York State and Connecticut. We sent flyers with Eva's photo to at least one hundred of them. One day, Ana received a call from a woman in New Jersey who was looking for a companion for her Doberman Pinscher. She lived way out in horse country, where houses were miles apart, and dogs hardly ever saw other canines for play dates. We made an appointment for the following weekend.

Marni, whose last name I've forgotten, was an inventor, a creative type with a dramatic bearing. She was tall and slim. To this day, I remember her eyebrows. They rose away from the bridge of her nose towards her hairline, like straightened bolts of lightning. Her dog, a red male, was named Reddy, a nice name, but about as original as "Rusty" and "Dobe" from my childhood. We went for a walk in the woods. Eva and Reddy ran loose, and, after sniffing one another, fanned out to investigate opposite sides of the path. Marni seemed to like Eva, but she wasn't sure about adopting her. She wanted time to think about it. She said she was hoping that Reddy would've engaged with Eva a bit greed to come back in two weeks. In the car going home, ‌ thought Marni's hesitation had to do with Eva's being a ‌ᴜᴎ. Despite what Marni had said, I thought so, too. It seemed like a waste of time to return, and it was. Although Reddy and Eva got along, Marni decided she wanted another Doberman. She thought he'd be happier with his own kind.

I took Eva back to Shelter Island in July, for the annual Blessing of the Animals at the Catholic Church. She wore her "adopt me" shirt which attracted attention, but no adopters. Meanwhile, Ana had contacted local newspapers both on and off the island. They ran a picture of Eva and me, along with a write-up describing what a great family pet Eva would make. My phone number and Ana's appeared as the contacts.

Eva stayed with the Schippies and me that week, in case someone in the area responded to the ad and wanted to see her. At night, she and Argo slept in wire crates, side by side in the bedroom, without making a sound. Monkey took her place on the pillow above my head, feeling superior to her crated cohorts. A few days later, a woman in Montauk called Ana and said she might be interested in adopting Eva. Then Ana called me. Kathy had a twelve year old mixed breed who was approaching the end of his time on earth, and she thought it might be good to get him a younger companion, and to also have one in place to fill the void when he died. We set up a date for the weekend, when Ana could get back to Shelter Island and meet Kathy in person.

In the meantime, I decided to train Eva to the Invisible Fence®. I set up the flags near the underground wire, and put on the receiver collar, which my other brother-in-law had given us when his big dog died the previous year. I told Eva to sit, and I snapped a flag on the ground, saying "No. Noooo." I didn't want to shock her. She was smart enough, I felt, to understand that she shouldn't go near the flags. Just then, a telephone repair crew pulled up to the pole in front of the house. Eva broke her sit and ran to investigate. Unfortunately, she chose the route where the wire was buried. To this day, I can hear her cries and she received shock after shock. She bolted across the road, out of range from this torture. I found her sitting under a bush, quivering. I spoke softly to her. Slowly, I crouched and approached her. In pain, or frightened, even the most mellow dog might bite. I sat down under the bush, next to her, and petted her. Then I removed the collar and left it on the ground. I tried to get her to stand and come with me, but she wouldn't budge. I didn't want to leave her to return to the house for her regular collar and lead. I was afraid she might run away. So, I picked her up. All 110 pounds of me carried this 45 pound Pit Bull back into the yard, back into the house. That ended Invisible Fence® training for Eva.

Kathy arrived on Shelter Island right on time and was introduced to Eva. Unlike Marni, who'd been hesitant, Kathy immediately fell in love with the dog. "She's gorgeous," she said.

I put Eva through some sits and downs, then took Eva up the little hill, past Mercury's grave. I told her to sit and stay. I returned to Ana and Kathy. Then I called the dog. She galloped towards me. I raised my arm, the flat of my hand making a "halt" signal. Eva executed a perfect front, facing me, sitting squarely about five inches from my feet. Monkey and Argo definitely could've taken a few lessons from her. Kathy was greatly impressed.

Ana had set up rules for Eva's adoption. One of them required a visit to the potential adopter's home. She wanted to see where the dog would eat and sleep, and make sure there weren't any hazards, such as unfenced yard on a busy road. Kathy had balked at this. She said she'd bring photos of her house and yard, but that it wasn't necessary for Ana to visit. Ana became suspicious that perhaps Kathy's home wasn't suitable, and she probably said something to that effect. Clearly, there was a chill in the hot summer air between these two women as they stood in my yard. I agreed with Ana about the visit, but I didn't want to see a potential adopter get away. Finally, I convinced her to let Kathy take Eva. The photos showed a modest house with a wooded property. It seemed fine.

Kathy signed the adoption agreement. It had the standard clause, that if, for any reason, the dog didn't work out, she was to be returned to Ana. In the middle of week, Ana received a phone call from Kathy. Her old mixed breed dog had attacked Eva, and although Eva wasn't seriously injured—just the tip of her ear had been bitten—Kathy knew it wasn't going to work. She drove Eva into the city and returned her to Ana.

Of course, Ana let me know that I was the one who had pressured her into letting Eva go to Kathy's without the home visit. If we'd have gone there, we might've noticed signs that the old dog wasn't going to accept her. I tried to tell Ana that it had been our best shot. Kathy was the only person who'd responded to the adoption write-up. I thought we had to be flexible. Ana saw it differently. She said from now on, a home visit was mandatory, otherwise *her dog* wasn't going anywhere.

Towards the end of the summer, a woman who worked for *Dan's Papers* where one of the write-ups had appeared, called Ana and said she had friends who might adopt Eva. They already had three Pit Bulls but would take her, if they all got along. Ana and I arranged to visit Marjorie and John, who lived in Riverhead, Long Island. Eva came with us. The couple had a double fenced yard, and John said he took the dogs to the beach in the early morning and let them run. This seemed the perfect home. John took each of his dogs out, one by one to sniff Eva on the street where I was waiting with her. Each walked a few paces with us, then returned to the house. By the time Eva entered the back yard, it was as if she'd been part of the pack forever. The dogs romped, fetched sticks, and every so often, came up to a human for a pat. "She's right at home," Marjorie said.

Ana and I stayed in touch with Marj and John over the years, and Ana often visited them. She also helped financially. After all, four Pit Bulls needed a lot of food and chew toys, plus veterinary care. I went along on a few of these outings. It was always a joy to see Eva. Then, two years after she'd been adopted, we learned that Eva had lymphoma. It was treatable but not curable. Eva could die within months. With chemo, she might have another year or so of life. Marj and John wanted to give her a chance, and John was willing to drive all the way to Southold every two weeks to the veterinary hospital where Eva would get treatment. Ana and I were torn. If Eva was going to die anyway, what was the point of treating her? We wondered if the treatments were painful, and if Eva would somehow understand they were for her own good. In the end, it was up to us, since Marj and John couldn't afford to pay for the treatments. Ana and I looked at each other, and then we looked at Eva. She was almost five years old. We couldn't condemn her to an early death. We told John and Marj to go ahead.

Eva enjoyed another two years of quality life. The last time I saw her, she was energetic, though a bit heavier due to the drugs she was taking. In the spring of 2007, Marj made two phone calls—one to me and one to Ana. The treatments no longer were working. Eva had stopped eating and she'd lost the happy gleam in her eyes. They made the heartbreaking decision and had her put down.

Chapter 16

September 11, 2001

In the fall of 2001, Bruce and I were headed to the Broadmoor in Colorado Springs. He was going to attend an annual bankers' convention, and happily, spouses were welcome. Each year, this event took place at a different luxury resort where tennis, golf, swimming, and of course, shopping provided diversions to those not attending seminars or working the room for new business. I had arranged for Anna, the dog walker, to stay in our apartment with Monkey and Argo. Our flight was due to take off from LaGuardia Airport at nine, so I walked the dogs beforehand, and told Anna she didn't need to take them out again until around three o'clock. I knew she had other dogs to walk.

It was a clear, crisp day, perfect for flying. LaGuardia, conveniently accessible by cab from where we lived at the time, was a mere twenty minutes away. But that morning, we took our car. The garage where we kept it was being painted, and we were afraid to come home to a splattered hood. Bruce had reserved a spot in the long term lot just outside the airport. It was a Tuesday, and we planned to return by the weekend. The date was September 11th.

We had boarded the aircraft and were sitting in our seats, waiting to taxi onto the runway when an announcement came over the loudspeaker. We were told to disembark, that there had been an incident requiring everyone to get off the plane. A collective moan erupted as people grabbed their gear from the overhead bins and quickly pulled out their cell phones. By the time we hustled through the jetway, we knew what had happened. A plane had crashed into the World Trade Center.

Inside the terminal, instead of breaking news, the television monitors showed golf tips. It was completely surreal. Just then someone in the crowd shouted that another airliner had hit the south tower of the trade center. Bruce and I were already nearing the escalator that led to the baggage claim. We scurried down the moving stairs. The carrousel was turning, and miraculously, our suitcases appeared. I pulled a twenty dollar bill from my wallet and told Bruce to move quickly and follow me. Normally, he walks at a much slower pace. Outside, crowds lined up at the taxi stand. Off to the left, I noticed a ramp. A few black cars and a couple of taxis headed our way.

"Come on," I yelled to him. I dragged my suitcase across the roadway and hailed one of the black cars. "Twenty bucks to take us to the long term lot," I said. The driver nodded. Normally, it would have cost less than half of that. We threw our luggage into the trunk. As the car crossed over the Grand Central Parkway, we could see the Manhattan skyline. In the distance, smoke billowed from the twin towers. It was hard to connect what we knew had happened to what we actually were seeing. By then, we'd learned that Manhattan had been locked down. No one, except emergency personnel, was allowed to enter. This meant we couldn't go home. We still didn't know the details of this catastrophe, so we decided to go to Shelter Island and spend a few hours at the house. From there, we'd call Anna and make sure she was on track with the dogs. We retrieved our car and headed east. As we passed one of the airport hotels, we saw at least a hundred people clustered outside, sitting on their luggage, perhaps waiting for alternative transportation. Many others were leaving the airport on foot, dragging their belongings behind them. Looking at them, at their grim and bewildered expressions, I realized how lucky we were that our garage had been slated for a paint job that day.

We reached Shelter Island shortly before noon. There was hardly any traffic. People who lived on Long Island but worked in the city still hadn't taken to the roads. There was a strange but eerie peacefulness to our trip. We kept the radio on. I was driving, and I asked Bruce to try Anna's number. We'd heard that all subway service had been suspended, and that no one could enter Manhattan by any means other than foot. Anna lived in Brooklyn. She couldn't drive in, and I knew she couldn't walk that distance. When we finally got through to her, she confirmed this.

I was worried about Monkey and Argo. By late afternoon, they'd need a walk. I thought about calling our doorman and asking him to take them out. He often walked dogs in the building. But this was no ordinary day; it was an emergency situation, and he might've been assigned other duties. I decided to call June, the young woman who took care of my elderly neighbor, Lillian. I tried for two hours, but the lines in area code 212 were busy. Finally, around 3:30, I got through. June had never walked Monkey and Argo, but she was willing to try. She had a key to our apartment, which I'd given her a few years ago, in case of an emergency. At the time, I never could have imagined a day like this. I told her where to find their collars and leashes, in the large wooden box that once served as a humidor. It sat on a long, marble-topped butcher block that extended the length of our hallway. I asked her to check their water, give them a few biscuits, and leave a light on in the apartment. She was welcome to keep them with her in Lillian's apartment, if they wanted to stay. I told her that somehow, we'd make it home that night.

Our car at the time was a grayish blue BMW 635CSI, a sleek, high performance coupe. The interior was tastefully done in blue gray leather, over which we'd put matching sheepskin seat covers. The "sixer," as we nicknamed it, could go 60 m.p.h. in second gear without hitting the red line. Bruce had bought it as a gift to himself when he completed his cancer treatments. To celebrate his return to life, he wanted something that went *varoom*.

We kept checking the news, trying to find out if the bridges were open, making Manhattan accessible once again. Every report we heard said it would be several hours before the all clear was issued, but this was the same information they'd been broadcasting since mid-afternoon. Shortly after six o'clock, we decided to leave for the city. Perhaps by the time we arrived at the Triborough Bridge, we'd get in. In hindsight, we should have left our luggage at the house. The "sixer's" trunk didn't accommodate both our large valises, so we had placed one of them on the back seat. Traveling light to these conventions was impossible. A person needed a varied wardrobe, from tennis or golf gear to dressy clothes, or jacket and tie for dinner.

We drove to the ferry terminal and had to wait several minutes for a boat to come over from the other side. Two ferry companies service Shelter Island. The North Ferry connects with Greenport, a former seafaring town whose main business today is tourism. At the opposite end of the island, South Ferry shuttles people to North Haven, and from there, they can continue to Sag Harbor and the Hamptons. Each operates independently of the other, which sometimes confuses day trippers and newcomers, who buy a round-trip, thinking it entitles them to take the other ferry.

We always used the North Ferry for our trips to and from the city. From Greenport, it's a thirty-five to forty-five minute drive to Riverhead, the town where the Long Island Expressway begins, or ends, depending on how one looks at it. That night, there was no traffic, and I reached Riverhead in half an hour. The Expressway, sometimes called the world's largest parking lot, was totally empty. There were no cars, no trucks, no buses. And no cops. At the edge of the grassy median in the center, a line of flares turned the roadway dark red. I assumed they'd been put there to guide emergency vehicles headed into the city. All local fire and police departments had responded to the tragedy. Knowing there were no police around to stop me, I drove that BMW the way it was designed to be driven on the autobahn in Germany. When I hit 100 miles per hour, I eased off to 90 and cruised at that speed in fifth gear for the rest of the way. My husband read a book the whole time. We arrived at the Queens border in under an hour, and then the run came to an abrupt end. Traffic was backed up the way it normally was on summer Sundays, when people who'd spent the weekend on eastern Long Island swarmed back into the city to face the work week. Bruce put down his book and pulled out a street map from the pocket inside the passenger's door. It was time to get off the Expressway and find some alternative routes.

All the side streets were bumper to bumper as well. I remember creeping along, and suddenly finding a street where I could accelerate to 30 m.p.h., then hitting another crunch of cars that forced me to stop for ten, maybe fifteen minutes without advancing an inch. No matter what routes my husband recommended, the results were the same—gridlock. Hours passed. It seemed as though we'd never make it to the Triborough Bridge. Once, I got close enough to one of the policemen directing traffic to ask him if he knew how we might get into Manhattan. He shook his head. "You can't," he said.

Saying "can't" to my husband is like saying "sit" to rabid dog bent on taking a chunk out of one's thigh. When I looked at the expression on his face, I knew we'd get home that night. He was familiar with back street shortcuts from his Friday trips to Shelter Island, so it made sense for him to take over the driving. He didn't need me to read the map. These routes were stored in his memory.

It was close to 11 p.m. when we finally made our way to the Triborough Bridge. There was a checkpoint at the access ramp, and a policeman was asking for identification. A few cars were in front of us, and we noticed that some were waved aside, while others were let onto the bridge. Bruce eased the "sixer" into the line. The officer asked where we thought we were going.

"Home," Bruce said. This made me reflect upon the irony of the situation. There'd been a smooth evacuation from Manhattan, but no

IN THE SHADOW OF MERCURY

one seemed to have considered the people who lived in that borough and had been caught outside when the tragedy struck. The police had not received any instructions as to how to deal with returning residents. This did not sit well with my husband. The officer asked if he was a doctor or any other type of medical professional. Bruce lied and said that he was.

"Identification, please," said the officer.

Bruce produced his health insurance card. The officer shook his head. At that moment, the car in front of us was waved clear. Bruce threw the "sixer" into first and hit the gas pedal. It was like a movie, except there was no chase. We were on the Triborough Bridge, headed home. I pictured Monkey and Argo, hungry, but happy the moment we arrived in the apartment. Our triumph was short lived. The police had set up a barricade at the exit to Manhattan. All vehicles on the bridge were being directed to the Bronx. It seemed pointless to plead our case with them.

We exited the bridge and headed north on the Major Deegan. From there, we could take the 138th Street exit and reach Manhattan via the Madison Avenue Bridge, which connected the Bronx with Harlem. But the only problem was, at the bridge, we encountered another roadblock. An officer stood between us and our needed route. Bruce lowered the window and asked if we could cross. The answer was no. I got out of the car and said that we lived in Manhattan, and that our dogs—I suppose I should've said children—had been without a caregiver the entire day. I emphasized that we needed to get home.

The officer was apologetic, and told us what we already knew, that only doctors and emergency personnel were allowed to drive into Manhattan. He suggested we park the car and cross the bridge on foot. I smiled at him, as if to say, "what a great idea." Leaving this shiny BMW with a suitcase on the back seat in that particular neighborhood was about as safe as placing a $10 bill on the sidewalk with a chalk-written sign saying, "don't touch."

If walking was the only way the authorities would let residents back into Manhattan, then I'd walk. I told Bruce I was going. He was on his own, and I wished him good luck. I needed to get home to the dogs.

I was one of the few people crossing the bridge over the Harlem River that night. On the other side, there were two ramps leading off the bridge, one to the left that ended on Madison Avenue, and one that led straight to Fifth Avenue. I chose the Fifth Avenue route, figuring I'd find the Number One bus cruising by. If I were lucky enough to catch it, I'd get a ride straight to the apartment. But that night there were no buses or cars. Streets that normally were bustling with traffic, now were eerily quiet. I could walk down the middle of any one of them and not have to worry about getting run over. It was 37 blocks, or about a mile and a half from 138th Street to my apartment building at 101st Street and Fifth Avenue. Walking at a brisk pace, I could make it in under an hour. A cluster of housing projects sat to the left of me as I started my hike. At this time of night, under normal circumstances, a woman alone might find herself at risk of getting attacked. But I didn't feel afraid. I saw a group of women standing in front of one of the buildings and I asked them if they had seen a Number One bus. They hadn't, but they did ask me what I was doing in the neighborhood at that hour. I told them what had happened and how I needed to get home to the dogs. One of the women fumbled in her purse and pulled out a card.

"Here's a taxi service," she said. "Maybe you can get a ride."

I thanked her and headed across the street to a pay phone. I had no cell phone at the time. And I had no luck with the cab. The line was constantly busy. I decided to keep walking. I passed a couple of young men dressed in baggy jeans and doo rags. At any other time, I might've kept my eyes on them, worried that they might try to grab my wallet, or stab me to death for fun, but that night, there was a strange solidarity in the air. The guys looked at me and continued on their way. As I approached 125th Street, a skinny, disheveled woman, smoking a cigarette, lurched towards me.

"Hey, honey, you know that guy over there? He's calling you."

I had no idea what she was talking about. I figured she was drunk or on drugs. She pointed towards the corner, and suddenly, I saw him, my knight in shining armor, with his valiant "steed," the "sixer." I thanked the woman and ran to the car.

"How'd you ever get into Manhattan?"

I thought, perhaps, they had finally opened the bridges, but no. After he left me, my husband had driven back to the Third Avenue Bridge, another Harlem River crossing less than half a mile away from where I had gotten out of the car. This time, he was ready for his health insurance card to be rejected. As soon as the officer handed it back to him, he hit the gas pedal and zoomed across the bridge. He knew no one was going to chase him. No one had orders on how to handle someone who dared to drive through the checkpoint.

"Good going," I said to him as he threw the "sixer" into gear. This was a desperate night that required desperate actions. Our Schipperkes were alone. They needed us. We looped around Mount Morris Park, an area fringed with old brownstones, renovated by rich yuppies, and continued down Fifth Avenue. The dark sky had a strange glow, like iridescent fog. The avenue was devoid of cars. Usually, they are parked on both sides of the street, and a city resident is lucky to find a space for an overnight. But that evening, it was like being in a movie, in one of those improbable scenes where the actors pull up in front of wherever they're going, and park, *just like that*, without having to circle the block twenty times. We saw a space right in front of our house. In fact, the entire avenue was one huge parking space. We grabbed the suitcases and headed for the lobby. The doorman came out and we embraced. He was thrilled to see us home safely. He took the bags and put them in the elevator. When we entered the apartment, Monkey and Argo raced to the door and jumped on us. I sat on the floor and let them lick and sniff me.

Bruce went to the bathroom while I affixed Monkey and Argo's collars. Then we took them out across the street for a short walk. When we returned, I fed them dinner. They inhaled it in seconds. Then we all went into the bedroom to sleep. It was one o'clock in the morning, on September 12th. We all were exhausted, but we had survived.

Manhattan was a ghost town the next morning. When I took the dogs out, no one I knew was in the park. Where had they gone, I wondered? Bruce had already packed the car when I returned from the shortened walk. It seemed wise to load up and get out. We headed back to Shelter Island. Unlike the previous night, there was no traffic in Queens, no congestion by the airport, and no need to drive at 90 miles per hour.

When we arrived on the island, I called a few friends who worked downtown. They all were safe. None had worked in the trade center, but they all had been near enough to hear the crash and to get covered with ash as they hurried out of their office buildings and embarked on the long trudge uptown to their apartments. One fellow, whom my husband knew from one of his first jobs on Wall Street, did work in the trade center, and sadly, he did not make it out alive.

The rhythm of Shelter Island changed dramatically after Labor Day. All the summer people's kids had gone back to school, and that meant their parents—my friends and tennis partners—had all gone home. The islanders' children were back in school, too. The beaches were empty, and the dog restrictions had been lifted. Monkey and Argo once again could race along the shore, chasing sea gulls and sniffing stinky piles of decaying seaweed. They were so full of life and energy. One time, long before 9/11, a pair of swans were gliding close to shore at our favorite beach, at the foot of Menhaden Lane. Monk and Argo charged towards them, barking ferociously, as they had done in our yard that time with the deer. Instead of heading out to sea, the swans emerged from the water and rose to their full height. They spread their wings and, like feathered monsters, advanced towards the Schipperkes. I have never seen a swan actually attack a dog or a human, but I'd heard that they can be quite nasty. Monkey and Argo must've sensed the same thing. They backed up, still barking, then turned and ran down the beach, leaving the swans to return to their swim.

Bruce went to his office on Friday. At that time he worked in New Jersey, so there was no risk of his being thwarted by detours or closed streets in Manhattan. I decided to stay on the island through the weekend. He planned to return Saturday morning. I rented a couple of movies, and knocked out a personal essay on my laptop about our adventures the night of 9/11. I sent it to the local paper, and it was published there along with a few other first person accounts.

By Sunday, it seemed safe to go back to the city. Daily life had resumed, but the pace of the city had changed. Downtown, the area below Canal Street was closed to the public for an unspecified time. All the companies that had offices there had moved their employees to temporary facilities, many of them just across the Hudson in New Jersey. The clean-up was bound to take months.

It was a strange time to be in Manhattan. Museums were empty, good restaurants had tables available at 8:00 p.m., and a person could walk at a New Yorker's pace through mid-town without getting stuck in tourist gridlock. Little by little, dog pals returned to the park. Many of them had, like us, fled to their country homes when the planes hit the towers. We traded stories. My trek through Harlem brought mixed reactions. Some people thought I was crazy, and others thought I was brave.

Chapter 17

Happy New Year

Right after Christmas, my husband and I flew to Paris. We had gone there the year before and had a fun time. In a way, we'd been forced. The Shelter Island chapter of the Nature Conservancy had, for many years, hosted a fabulous New Year's Eve party in the manor house of the Mashomack Preserve. But as of the year 2000, they stopped having the event, leaving us with nothing to do for New Year's. Paris seemed like a good alternative.

We left Monkey and Argo with my friend, Grace, on Long Island. She was a terrific cook, and she always gave them forbidden treats. Plus, she had a big house. They bounded through the rooms like schoolchildren at recess. This was a good thing. They needed exercise, but she didn't have a fenced yard, so they had to be satisfied with indoor racing. Outside, she always used their leashes.

On that first New Year's trip, as 2000 tipped into 2001, Paris was alive with lights and crowds and a city-wide celebratory feeling. This was their millennium, unlike ours which took place when the clock struck midnight on January 1, 2000. We had decided to shun the four star hotel dinner and dancing scene and find something out of the way and interesting. The day before, I had eaten a *crêpe* from a street vendor, and the topping that I chose was tainted, although it didn't taste off. I ended up with a stomach that rivaled Mt. Etna's eruptions. So, on New Year's Eve, I was hoping, praying for a miraculous recovery. I sent Bruce to visit a couple of the places we'd found in *Time Out Paris* and decide if any one of them might make for a quirky and fun-filled evening. Though he didn't speak French, he had a way of making himself understood. He chose a restaurant in an Arab quarter, near the *Gare du Nord,* accessible by *métro.* Though it was last minute, they had room for two more people. By evening, luckily, I was cured. I put on a strappy dress and off we went. No one in the restaurant spoke English, which was o.k. by me. Remember, I'd been a French major. But Bruce had to make do with gestures and smiles. It was easy, since the "couple" seated to his right were two women who giggled good naturedly at his attempts to communicate.

There was a small dance floor, and an even smaller band. Actually it was a fellow with a keyboard that played a variety of danceable tunes. We had a fine French dinner, venison, I believe it was, and the accompanying wines flowed all evening. We knew that the *métro* shut down at 1 a.m., but when we finally checked the time, it was fifteen minutes past that. We decided to leave anyway. Perhaps we could find a cab. We walked three blocks to the *Gare du Nord.* It was drizzling. A huge crowd clustered outside. Some people were standing, others were sitting on their luggage or backpacks. They were all waiting for the trains to start running again at five in the morning. One man told us he'd walked all the way from the Eiffel Tower. He couldn't get a taxi. As it turned out, neither could we. After trying, fruitlessly, for twenty minutes, we decided to return to the restaurant.

By 3:30 a.m., the last of the revelers left the restaurant. The one-man band packed his things. We asked the proprietor if he knew of any cab companies we might call, or if he had a friend or relative who might drive us home, for a fee. He said no. But he told us, if we didn't mind waiting until the staff ate their New Year's dinner and cleaned up, he himself would take us back to our hotel. We had no choice. We returned to our table. Bruce put his head down and dozed. I, too, nodded off for a while. It was almost five in the morning when the proprietor announced he was ready to leave. We followed him out and watched as he pulled down the metal gate in front of the restaurant. His van was parked out front, and he, his twelve year old son, who had helped out as a waiter during the evening, Bruce and I all climbed into the front seat. I told him the name of the small hotel where we were staying, but he didn't recognize it. Luckily, I remembered a large department store nearby, and I said I could help him find the hotel from there. When we finally pulled up in front of the *Hôtel Sèvres-Saint Germain,* we thanked him and offered to reimburse him for gas. But he said, no. We shook hands and said good-bye. It was the latest my husband and I had ever stayed up since our college days.

As much fun as that New Year's was, this second trip was the exact opposite. This time we chose a Cuban restaurant near the *rue Saint Denis.* It was larger than the Arab restaurant, but its dance floor was about the same size. This meant each couple had about two square feet of space. We arrived around 11 p.m., thinking the place would be bursting with Latino rhythms and festively dressed patrons. Instead, we found an older than middle-aged crowd and a band that played tunes that could put folks to sleep. I don't remember what was served for dinner, but I do recall that it wasn't very good. We left at one minute past midnight and took the *métro* home.

The New Year's Eve after that was even worse. We spent it with Don and Linda, a couple we'd met on one of our trips. In the spring of 2002, my husband and I had traveled to Cuba on a totally legal cultural exchange. We'd gone with a group from the Joyce Theatre in New York, a venue that hosts geographically diverse dance troupes throughout its performance season. Though most of us were middle-aged travelers and not dancers by any reach of the imagination, we were allowed access to this Communist capital in the name of the arts. This was before the Bush administration clamped down on what types of groups would be allowed to go on such excursions. Back then, our days and nights there were filled with one or more dance related activities—going to clubs to dance and drink with the locals, visiting a studio to see students perform, attending formal receptions with lectures on dance, and seeing professional dancers on stage in both modern and folkloric presentations. We felt truly elite since most Americans who wanted to go to Cuba and couldn't figure out a way to attach themselves to a "cultural exchange" program, had to slip into the country through Canada or Mexico, something we never would have considered. Despite our 9/11 actions, we were law abiding folks.

Don and Linda, like many of the Joyce travelers, lived in New York City. We enjoyed their company and promised to stay in touch once the trip was over. In the fall, we visited them at their town house, which was around the corner from the Joyce. When the holidays came, Don and Linda invited us to a New Year's Eve party at the National Arts Club on Gramercy Park. This historic private home was built in the 1840's and became known as the Tilden mansion after Samuel Tilden bought it in the 1860's and "updated" it in the 1870's in Victorian style. Today, it is a National Historic Landmark, with an interior that recalls a bygone era. This seemed an ideal place to ring in the New Year. It could have been, except that, somewhere in the middle of the evening, my husband disappeared. While other couples were dancing, I sat at our table. Our hosts, Don and Linda, asked several times where he was, and I had to admit, I didn't know. Twice, I made a tour of the club at the level where the dinner festivities were being held, thinking perhaps he had seen someone he knew and sat down with them for a drink. But I didn't find him.

The band rang in the New Year. Don and Linda danced, and I sat alone at the table. When our hosts returned, I thanked them for a lovely evening and went downstairs to get my coat. It was then that I spotted Bruce. He was emerging from a room in the back that was designated for cigar smokers. I glared at him. He appeared drunk as he approached me as if nothing out of the ordinary had happened. I told him to go screw himself. I redeemed my coat, and shrugged off his attempt to help me put it on. With that, I walked out into the night, into a new year.

Of course, there were no cabs, so I took the subway home. It was populated with people wearing jeans and parkas. These were workers, not revelers, and I recall feeling sorry for them, for the fact that they had to work while everyone else was having a good time, supposedly. I think I was a little bit drunk myself, because I remember thinking, if anyone in that subway car had shown me the least bit of kindness, I would've kissed him—or her, and perhaps gone out for a drink, if asked. But just like my husband, no one paid any attention to me. When the train arrived at 96th Street, I got out. Though tipsy, I was not foolish enough to get off at the closer station, 103rd Street, and risk walking past the projects on New Year's.

I didn't get up when Bruce came home. I heard him, but I pretended to be asleep. I was too tired to have a row at that hour of the night. The next morning was gray and drizzly. It was a perfectly gloomy start to what was to become a perfectly gloomy year in our marriage. I slipped on my raincoat and took Monkey and Argo out for their walk. Few people were in the park at 8 a.m. The first day of the new year is always like that. In fact, it's the best day to see a popular movie at its first showing, before the crowds come, and that's exactly what I did. When I returned with the dogs, Bruce was drinking coffee. He tried to apologize, but I had no interest in what he had to say. Cold silence, rather than words, would express how disgusted I was with his behavior. I looked up the movie schedule, grabbed my coat, and walked through the park to the West Side.

I don't recall what the movie was, but like much of what went on for the next two months, it didn't matter. My husband and I co-existed. We were polite, but distant. At dinner, we sat at the same table, each of us locked in silence. Neither spoke about the New Year's Eve party, nor did we say much else, except for things like, "pass the carrots, please." The dogs sensed that something was wrong. They ignored Bruce and gave all their attention to me.

One night, about a month later, we were going out to dinner downtown. The restaurant was in an area not accessible by subway or bus, so it made no sense to take a $40 round trip cab ride. Bruce left to get our car, which was parked a few blocks away. Usually, I waited in the lobby of our building, but this time, I decided to walk to the next block. I saw him round the corner onto Fifth Avenue. There was no traffic that Sunday night, and nobody on the streets. I stepped off the curb and flailed my arms. He drove right past me. I rushed back to our building as the doorman was explaining to him that I'd gone to meet him outside. In happier times, I might have laughed it off and called him unconscious. But coming shortly after the New Year's Eve fiasco, it hit me quite differently. I was invisible to him and I'd had enough.

In early March, I packed up my gear, loaded Monkey and Argo into the car, and left for Shelter Island.

Chapter 18

Island Life

Shelter Island off season is astonishingly quiet. One might even call it spooky. Like many city dwellers alone in a house and new to nature, I slept lightly at first, and the tiniest sound awakened me. Raccoons, when they attacked the lawn, searching for grubs, made a soft rasp with their claws, and this muffled noise knew the exact path to my bedroom. Deer, though silent in their foraging, aroused the dogs' sensitivities, and when these critters visited the yard at night, the Schipperke's watchdog instincts kicked in. Barking erupted. At first, I'd go downstairs, put on the outside lights and let them out. I figured they'd chase any wildlife out of the yard, and if, by chance, there was an escaped mental patient or ax murderer lurking, they'd scare him off, too. But after a few days of interrupted sleep, I stopped doing this. It had become a game for them. After two or three more nights of ignoring them and telling them to be quiet, they settled down, and so did I.

I started writing a novel. Like my rejected romance novels, it had a snappy title: *On the Six Train at Midnight with Jackie O.* My New Year's Eve trip home on the subway inspired this work. I might have mentioned before that I had always been a fan of Jackie Kennedy Onassis. Fueled by the wine I had drunk at the party, I imagined that the young woman standing across from me in the car was dressed in a "first lady," outfit, complete with pillbox hat and gloves, instead of jeans and a parka. When a seat opened next to me, I imagined she took it. Since we were the only two people wearing festive attire, I also imagined that we exchanged a few pleasantries. From there, I crafted a story. It was somewhat autobiographical, and of course the husband character was based on mine. I never finished the book, but it kept me busy and energized during those quiet, solitary months on Shelter Island. I wrote in the mornings after taking Monkey and Argo to the beach for a romp. If it was early enough, shortly after dawn, we saw deer, and they chased them. We returned home and I worked for a while, until it was time to go to the Post Office.

Shelter Island doesn't offer home delivery of mail, perhaps because of its amoeba-like shape, which makes getting from *here* to *there* a bit tricky and time consuming. Everyone goes to one of two post offices, the Heights or the Center. When we had rented the house in Dering Harbor, we took out a box at the Heights, and, although the house we bought is a short bike ride to the Center, we kept our address at the Heights. Every morning, around 10 a.m., I'd put the dogs in the car and drive to the post office. By then, the mail had been distributed and my *Wall Street Journal* had arrived. At that hour, it was also a safe bet that the other newspapers had landed at the Shelter Island Pharmacy. Both places displayed small town charm. The employees were friendly and they knew me by name, along with everybody else. This was annoying if one were in a hurry, and the person in front was crowing about her latest grandchild, (and it was always a *her* who was yakking). But I realized soon enough that I had no reason to rush, so I slipped into the lazy rhythms of the tranquil off-season.

Mornings passed quickly. I read the papers, then puttered around outdoors, clearing dead plants from the garden, pruning bushes, or cleaning out the shed. I was surprised that I found these activities satisfying.

In the afternoon, I wrote a bit more, checked email and took the dogs for a run on the trails at the horse farm down the street from our house. Paard Hill, *paard* meaning horse in Dutch, had been built a few years earlier amidst great controversy. Originally a private home with vast acreage, the sellers faced a choice: sell to the horse people or sell to a developer. Some neighbors whose properties abutted the farm, tried to prevent the sale. They feared manure and flies. Silly people. The grounds and stables of this "barn," easily could have graced a glossy, coffee table magazine showcasing luxury housing for horses. The stalls were spotless and the residents, pampered. Strangely, no one rode the trails, preferring to take lessons or hack in one of the many outdoor rings, or inside, in the covered arena. This was great for me and my dogs. As soon as we arrived at the head of the trail, I'd release Monkey and Argo. They flew ahead of me, like two black rockets, chasing rabbits, deer, and once, a red fox. Yet they never bothered the horses in the pasture. It's been said that Schipperkes have a natural respect

111

for horses, and from my observations, this proved true. Paard Hill's owner gladly gave me access to his posted land since I was one of the first signers of the petition in support of his farm.

Around 6:30, I'd have dinner—usually a piece of fish or steak and a salad, plus two or three glasses of wine. Then I wrote some more. Sometimes I rented a movie, and usually I was in bed, asleep, by 9:30 or 10. I got up around 5, and as soon as the grayish light of a new day appeared over the treetops, I let the dogs out and started the routine once again. It was soothing to have no commitments and to lead a simple life for a change. I stayed in touch with my city friends by email, and sometimes by phone. I had told them that I just needed to get away for a while.

None of my summer tennis friends had arrived on the island, so I hopped over to East Hampton Indoor and joined a weekly league. We played women's doubles and most of the players were at least at my level or better. This was pretty much the only contact I had with people during the week, except for the post office, the pharmacy and the video store. I wasn't lonely. I had Monkey and Argo. I also had an accordion.

During my dalliance with possible mid-life careers, I had taken up my childhood instrument. I imagined myself playing in subway stations, happily accepting donations from passersby as they waited for the train. I had found a 120 bass accordion on eBay, as a "buy it now" item, and since it was inexpensive, I bought it. Bruce picked it up from the seller in New Jersey on his way home from work one evening. He lugged it into the living room. When I opened the case, the scent of mildew hit my nose, like a punch. Monkey and Argo each took a few sniffs and backed away. I picked up the accordion and slipped my arms through the straps. The instrument was heavy and big, the way 120 bass accordions are supposed to be, and it dwarfed me. Its outer shell was sky blue pearlized plastic, and above the keyboard, in ornate script, appeared the brand name. Crucinelli. I hit a few notes. The dogs fled down the hall. My husband snickered. And I laughed as well. My mother had often referred to the accordion as a "groan box," and that nickname fit this instrument perfectly. I played a scale, and as I opened the bellows, gravelly sounds emerged. Clearly I needed a better accordion.

I never played in the subway, but I did get a 48 bass accordion from a shop downtown on Essex Street, called the Main Squeeze. It was run by a German guy who played in a band, and also gave lessons. The lessons, I soon discovered, were a way to audition women for his all female accordion orchestra that appeared at funky clubs on the lower East Side and in Brooklyn. After a few months of weekly lessons, he concluded that I showed no promise, but it didn't matter. I wasn't interested in joining his group. It would have required a huge time commitment, even if I had been talented enough to have been selected. By then, I had learned a few tunes such as "Skip to My Lou," "Beautiful Brown Eyes," and a selection of Christmas carols. I played them for my neighbor Lillian every so often. These were old timer's tunes, and her eyes brightened with recognition as she happily sang along.

I brought the Crucinelli to Shelter Island. When I played, it rested heavily on my thighs. I was sure I was going to turn black and blue. In the quiet of the island, I practiced every afternoon for about half an hour, often playing "Dixie," which I had learned by heart. The accordion growled and Monkey and Argo retreated, just as they had in the apartment, the first time they heard my amateurish attempts at playing music. After my session, I announced, in an extra loud voice, "Accordion's finished," and they came racing back into the living room, an almost human expression of relief flickering across their little canine faces.

I had mastered "Dixie" and a few other southern tunes that required sheet music, in order to entertain my friend Dorothy and her husband. They'd moved to Virginia from Bedford, New York, after he retired. For years, Dorothy had been my riding buddy and confidante. We had met at Fox Hill Farm in Pleasantville, not far from Armonk, where she lived at that time. I was in my mid-forties then and Dorothy was a year or two older. We both took lessons on school horses and rode the trails on the adjacent Rockefeller estate. That was before the family donated the land for use as a state park. Those were magical days, akin to a trip back in time. On one ride, we saw the elder Mrs. Rockefeller's coach, pulled by four white horses, on the far side of the lake. Mist rose from the water, creating an effect straight out of a Merchant Ivory film. The trails were perfectly groomed, probably to make sure the grande dame's coach didn't throw a wheel, but it benefited us. We could gallop uphill or canter for long stretches without fear of our horses stumbling on debris.

There was a dairy on the estate, complete with cows that mooed, and sometimes the horses spooked as we passed. This turned an ordinary pleasure ride into a test of our horsemanship. Luckily we never got dumped. It would have been at least a two hour walk back to Fox Hill, if the panicked horse had raced home. After our rides, we'd go back to Dorothy's house for lunch and trade stories. Each of us felt diminished by our husbands. Hers, it turned out, was similar to mine. They both hoarded old newspapers, both had solid careers with good incomes, and both were men of few words when it came to relationships, except to make negative remarks. I remember telling Dorothy about the first time one of my articles was published in a magazine. I was thrilled, and the moment my husband came home, I told him. I thought he'd at least say, "That's great. Let's have a look." But instead he chose to open his mail. From that day on, I never shared any of my writing with him. As for Dorothy, she had left the workforce, too, after a series of cutbacks in the travel industry, which was her field. Our husbands made us feel that unless we were bringing home $30,000 to $40,000 a year (a lot of money in those days), we weren't considered equals.

Eventually, Dorothy's husband bought her a horse, an energetic paint mare, and they moved from Armonk to Bedford. I'd often drive up to meet her after her riding lesson and we'd walk the trails adjacent to her new barn, a charming place, which unfortunately, offered no horses for hire. By then, I had acquired Mercury, and Dorothy had two black Labs she'd nicknamed the gorilla girls. We'd let them off lead to explore while we walked and complained about our husbands' insensitivity.

Dorothy was six feet tall and I was five three. Together, we were an odd pairing. On the ground, I'd have to tilt my head up to talk to her, but on horseback we were almost level. I missed riding with her, so once a year, I'd drive down to the old plantation they'd bought, and were restoring, and we'd hop on her horses and go. Though these rides were enjoyable, they were tame compared to the galloping and cross country jumping we did when we rode hunter pace or went fox hunting together. Dorothy had vanned her mare down to Virginia. Then she added a pony and another, younger steed, so there was always something for me to ride. At Rokeby, which was the name of their Civil War era plantation, days were lazy and nights, quiet. It was clear that my visits and accordion concerts were one of the high points of their country squire lifestyle. There was nothing to do in the evenings other than watch television or rented movies. Restaurants, unless they were in the mall, closed by eight o'clock.

Dorothy died in March 2006, at age 64, after a nine month bout with melanoma. I flew to Washington then drove the rest of the way for her funeral. She was buried at the plantation, alongside the pony and her mare, who had been put down the year before because of illnesses stemming from old age. I've not traveled that way since, nor have I given any more accordion concerts to anyone, anywhere. But I still can play "Dixie" by heart.

*   *   *

Bruce came out for the weekend after I'd been on Shelter Island for two weeks. We were cordial to each other, but there was no attempt,

114

by either one of us, to talk about what was wrong or how we might fix it. For my part, I figured it wouldn't do any good, and he probably felt the same way. So we continued our silent dinners, sometimes adding a word here or a sentence there.

"Good fish," he might say.

"They said it was caught this morning," I'd reply. And that was that.

I slept on the sofa in the living room. It was narrow and there wasn't enough room for Monkey to snooze on my pillow, so she and Argo made themselves comfortable on the floor.

Bruce didn't come out every weekend, but when he did, we continued our peculiar ways. Eventually, I returned to the upstairs bedroom. The sofa, an antique bench style, was upholstered and cushioned, but nowhere as comfortable as a real mattress. After a while, we started saying good night to each other, or more precisely *bonne nuit*, an affectation we'd embraced eons ago, on our first trip to France together in the late 1970s.

During that summer, we attended the usual Shelter Island fundraisers for the East End Hospice, the Historical Society, the Nature Conservancy's Mashomack Preserve and St. Gabriel's Center for Youth. Most of these were cocktail parties or buffets, which was good. We mingled with other people and didn't have to sit next to each other at a table, with pasted-on smiles, and pretend we were happy as clams.

Chapter 19

Zorra and Lucy

In September, I returned to the city. It hardly felt as if I'd been gone six months. The time had passed quickly, uneventfully, and pleasantly, even when my husband came out for weekends. By the end of the summer, we were pretty much back to the way we'd been before that horrid New Year's Eve, cordial to each other, but also emotionally distant.

On crisp fall days, I strolled around the neighborhood, checking out rental buildings that allowed dogs. I toyed with the idea of getting my own place and ending our weird charade once and for all. But as I said earlier, my husband wasn't a bad person. To the best of my knowledge, he never fathered a slew of kids out of wedlock, nor did he keep a young woman on the side. He drank wine and beer, and smoked cigars, but that was it for his vices. So, after looking around and finding every place unsuitable, I shelved that plan. All of the buildings were at least three blocks from the park, much too far when one was used to living directly across from it. Plus, and I observed this while lurking near these buildings, dogs had to go in and out through the service entrances. This brought back memories of the nasty fellow who used to live at our place and who wanted me to use the back elevator with my pets. It didn't take much soul-searching. I decided to stay.

A friend of mine had a New Year's Eve party that year. It was a small gathering in her apartment, with good food and wine, and no unmarked corridors into which a husband could disappear for an hour or so without telling his wife. At a few minutes to midnight, we all stood in front of the television and watched the ball drop. We drank a

Champagne toast, and by one a.m., everyone had headed home. That was how middle-aged New Yorkers whooped it up.

In February, I turned 60. It was hard to believe ten years had passed since that sad affair with Mercury. I thought about him from time to time, but I had Monkey and Argo now, and life was good once again. To celebrate this big birthday, Bruce hosted a party for me in the private dining room of the Gramercy Tavern, one of our favorite restaurants. It was a mid-day luncheon, with a small group of friends, good wine and great food, plus music. I had hired an accordion player whom I'd seen at various venues around town. She filled the room with soft, fluid melodies—no polkas or "Lady of Spain—playing the way I wished I could play. It was a great party, and friends still remember it to this day. As a gift, one which I had requested, my husband endowed a bench in Central Park. The plaque reads: Happy Birthday, Melanie. From Bruce and the Schipperkes. February 15, 2004. I chose the location because it's on my morning route with the dogs, just north of the baseball fields on the upper pathway, near a big, old tree.

I don't remember much else about that winter, whether we had snow, and if so, whether I cross-country skied in Central Park, or brought out my little bob sled and slid down the hills near our apartment. Many people keep journals, but after my teenage years, I abandoned that form of writing. My naughty younger sister had found my diary one time, and amused herself for an entire afternoon reading about my crushes on unattainable hunks, plus my comments on teachers whose classes she had yet to take. A journal was risky, but I wished I had one to fill in the gaps.

Spring 2004 required no such memory jogger. I can remember everything as if I were reading it off a printed page. Ana called me one afternoon. Eva was still alive at the time, living with Marj and John, and my first thought was that something had happened to her. But Eva was fine. It was two homeless females, Zorra and Lucy, who needed help. Their owner had died, and Ana, along with other animal-friendly people in her neighborhood, had taken in the woman's pets. Ana asked if I would help her find homes for these two dogs, and of course I said yes.

Lucy looked like a mix of a Basset Hound and Beagle, with a touch of Cocker Spaniel stirred in. She was terribly overweight and it seemed as if her stumpy Basset's legs might collapse at any moment from the burden of supporting her body. She was docile and sweet tempered. When I looked into her eyes I saw a yearning to be loved.

Zorra, we thought, was a black Lab mix, although the ASPCA, where Ana had had her examined and vaccinated, wrote on her chart, "Doberman mix." As an experienced dog person, I knew that was wrong the moment I saw her. If anything, she resembled a Dalmatian, except she was black with a white patch on her chest. I figured she had some Pit Bull in her, too, since she had come from the streets. The woman who had died, had found Zorra as a stray in East Harlem and had taken her in. We didn't know how this woman had acquired Lucy, but the point was, the two of them needed homes.

I agreed to walk Zorra and Lucy in the afternoons, since Ana was working, and the only dog walker available in her neighborhood had a demanding drug habit. Ana refused to use him. She was afraid he'd sell the dogs for a hit. I still had the keys to her house from the time I helped her with Eva. The first day I went to take them out, the moment I put the key in the door, barks exploded. It wasn't the kind of barking that said, "Get out of here or we'll bite your butt off," but it wasn't that welcoming either. Slowly I opened the door. Lucy stood in front of it, woofing like a hound on a rabbit scent, but anyone trying to enter, who looked at her face, knew she was no threat. Zorra stood further back in the room. Her scruff was up and she seemed jittery. I spoke to Lucy and made myself small by getting down on all fours to greet her. She came to me. I stroked her head and scratched her under the chin. She wagged her tail. I got up and took the leash and collar off the peg where Ana had hung them. Then I turned to Zorra. She had hopped up on the bed and was staring at me with bared teeth. "Go away, or I'll bite you," her expression said.

I sat down on the floor again and petted Lucy. Every few seconds, I'd look at Zorra. I spoke to her, telling her she was a good girl, and that if she let me come closer, we'd go out and have a fun time. She watched me with her black onyx eyes. I rose and took her collar off the peg. When I approached to put it on, she bared her teeth again. This continued for a long stretch of time. I'd approach, she'd shy away or show teeth, I'd go back to the floor with Lucy, and then I'd try again. An hour passed. Finally Zorra allowed me to get close enough so I could put the collar on. It took another five minutes to attach the leash. She kept bounding away from me, from the bed to the sofa, then back again to the bed, as if her legs were springs. I kept speaking softly to her, and when at last, she let me clip on the leash, I took them both outside. Somehow, lumbering Lucy made it down the steps, which led from the front door to the sidewalk. I hoped she could make it back up. She was too heavy for me to carry.

Ana had laid down newspapers at one end of the bedroom for the dogs to do their business. Before she called me, there had been no midday walk for the "girls." Zorra, I would learn in time, was intuitively smart, and she figured the newspapers were the only place where she was supposed to "go." I walked her and Lucy around the block. It was like walking a sea lion and a cheetah, though Lucy, the sea lion, knew how to make use of the sidewalk. Of course, I brought bags for cleaning up. Zorra walked like a panther, slinky and furtive, and she appeared anxious to get home. The moment I unclipped the leash, she went straight to the paper.

Ana and I made four-color flyers with photos of each dog. I'd taken them one afternoon in the park, using an instant camera. I was pleased with the outcome. Both "girls" looked friendly and adoptable. But I cautioned Ana that Zorra might be a hard sell since most people who live in apartments don't want a big dog that does its business on newspapers indoors. I promised to continue to work with her. As we'd done with Eva, we sent flyers to veterinarians' offices, and posted them in the dog-friendly bookstore on Madison Avenue. We kept to the better neighborhoods, hoping that someone with a country home might take one or both of the dogs, so they could enjoy weekends and summers away. I continued to work with Zorra. I decided she needed longer walks and more individual attention, so first I'd take both her and Lucy around Ana's block, then I'd drop off Lucy, and take Zorra to the park. I was amazed that Lucy managed to waddle up those front steps. Her stomach swept each one.

I walked Zorra on the bridle path in the park, thinking that the smell of horses might encourage her to "go." One day, after weeks of covering this terrain, she squatted and peed. "Good girl," I shouted, clapping my hands and letting her jump on me in response to my enthusiasm. I received a few strange looks from other strollers, but they couldn't have understood what a triumph this was. Ana had arrived home by the time we returned. She had good news of her own. A woman had called in response to the flyer at the bookstore. She said she'd like to meet Lucy.

We made a date for the next day and arranged to meet in the park. For Lucy, this meant traveling two crosstown blocks, but to a dog in her shape, it probably felt like cross country. It took almost half an hour to get there. The woman, Amy, was a well-known writer and teacher and she liked Lucy immediately. Yet she wasn't ready to pick up the leash and take the dog home with her. Her lecture schedule often took her out of town, and after thinking about it for a week, she decided not adopt Lucy.

The veterinarians who had seen both dogs surmised that Lucy was anywhere from six to eight years old and that Zorra was about two. With Lucy's weight and age, we figured the best home might be with an equally large, older person, someone who didn't like exercise. Zorra, on the other hand, needed lots of activity. It was impossible, we realized, to adopt them out together.

I told Ana I'd take Zorra on my morning walk with Monkey and Argo. That way I could show her off to other dog people in the park. From nine at night until nine in the morning, except for the interim hours when the park was supposedly closed, dogs were allowed to run free in certain areas of Central Park. If Zorra romped with some of these dogs, and if their owners saw how congenial she was, perhaps they'd consider adding her to their household. I stuffed a batch of flyers into my fanny pack. On the bridle path, near where the Central Park jogger had been assaulted years before, I spotted a police scooter. I gave the officer a flyer and asked if she'd post it at the precinct. I pointed to Zorra. "This is the dog in the photograph. She's wonderful, and she needs a home."

No officer ever responded regarding Zorra, but a woman in northern Manhattan did. She had seen Zorra's picture on PetFinder, where someone Ana knew had arranged to place it. The woman had a young daughter, about 7 years old, too young, we thought to walk a dog of Zorra's high energy by herself. The mother worked outside the home, returning around 6 o'clock. This seemed far from ideal, so Ana and I took a subway ride to the neighborhood. The nearby park was a repository of debris, an eyesore compared to the groomed serenity of Central Park. It was a mere two square blocks in size, and busy streets bordered the periphery. Before we even met the woman, we decided this was not the right environment for Zorra. We called and lied, saying that Zorra had found a home.

My husband drove Zorra and me to Riverside Park, on the west side of Manhattan, near the Hudson River. This park had enclosed dog runs, and a whole new population of dog owners. Perhaps this was the place where Zorra would find a new home. I posted a flyer at the run and introduced Zorra to some of the people. I let her off lead. She sniffed at some dogs, but didn't engage in play. The other dogs didn't seem all that interested in her. After an hour, people left for work and Zorra and I began the long trudge home.

A short time later, and I can't recall how it came about, I was contacted to put Zorra on a pet adoption cable tv show. This meant heading over to Riverside Park once again, in the early evening, where the shoot was scheduled to take place. I think we took a cab there and walked back. I'm not sure. With the Hudson River shimmering in the background against a setting sun, I told Zorra's story on camera and spoke of her great personality. I gave my phone number and urged people to add this wonderful dog to their family. Days passed and I received no calls.

Walking and training Zorra, plus taking care of Monkey and Argo filled my days from mid-afternoon through early evening. After a while, I felt overburdened. At night, my husband and I often went to the ballet, or out to dinner, and I had a calendar filled with theatre and movie dates with my women friends. This meant I had to rush home from Zorra, walk and feed my dogs, shower, get dressed and travel to the restaurant or venue where I had arranged to meet my husband or pals. I knew I couldn't do this much longer. I had become short-tempered and surly. Yet I couldn't abandon Ana, Lucy and Zorra. It was time to take the adoption campaign to Shelter Island.

Ana now trusted me enough to agree with my plans for Zorra. With Eva, it was always touch and go. Ana thought she knew better, whereas, in reality, as a cat person and first time dog owner, she knew nothing about training at all. It had been a long, slow process to win her over to the fact that Eva was a dog, not a person, and that dogs, with their inherent pack orientation, had to be handled differently than, for example, children. She used to drive me crazy with her questions, challenging every aspect of my work with Eva.

"Why don't you let her jump on you?" she might say, "That shows that she's happy."

Then I'd have to explain why a 45 pound dog, leaping up on a person, could cause someone to fall and get injured. "Law suits, Ana," I'd reply. "She's a Pit Bull. Do you want her taken away?"

Little by little, as she saw the results with Eva, she began to rethink her positions. Over time, we formed a sturdy friendship, though it still included occasional spats thanks to her Latin temper.

When I asked Ana if I could bring Zorra to Shelter Island for a few days, she said yes. We still had some flyers left over, so I grabbed them and put them into my bag. In the apartment, I moved the crates from the den into the hallway, a sign to Monkey and Argo that a trip lay ahead. Then I went to fetch Zorra. My car was parked on 103rd Street, a half block out of the way if I'd wanted to go straight home. But I figured, since I had Zorra with me, it made more sense to get the car, drive to the apartment, then go up for the Schipperkes and crates while the doorman kept an eye on my vehicle.

When I opened the tail gate, Zorra hopped into the back of my Subaru wagon. She seemed happy to experience something new and I watched as she gave a good sniff to the cargo area. We had installed a pet screen that kept an animal from leaping over onto the back seat, and at the last minute, just before I was about to get into the driver's seat, I decided to make sure it was securely fastened. I opened the trunk lid. Zorra, in high energy mode, flew out of the car onto the street. My heart plunged.

A half block away was Central Park with its enticing greenery, a perfect destination for a dog on the loose. But to get there, she would have to cross Fifth Avenue. At that hour, cars and buses, intent on getting to their destinations in the city, might not stop in time to avoid a crazed black dog savoring a dizzying burst of freedom.

I called her. She had bounded into the middle of the street. Some men, hopefully not doctors, were smoking cigarettes outside the Academy of Medicine on the corner. They snickered among themselves then laughed out loud as they watched, enthralled with Zorra's antics. It was also clear they had no clue as to the dangers that faced her.

I yelled at them. "You wouldn't think it's so funny if she got hit by a car."

Luckily there was no traffic on 103rd Street that morning, and Zorra did not run to the park. I clapped my hands and called her but she continued her ballet in the middle of the street. I ran down the block away from her, cooing her name. Luckily, that worked. She followed me, and when she came close enough for me to grab her collar, I did. I led her back to the car and she hopped in. I petted her. "Zorra with me", I said as I scratched her chest, then patted my own. "With me."

We had installed a split rail fence around our property on Shelter Island. It had wire mesh between the ground and the first course, more to keep out stray dogs than to keep the Schipperkes in. Monkey and Argo knew the boundaries, thanks to years with the Invisible Fence®. Both Bruce and I had become tired of the costly repairs required at least once a season. Apparently moles or other digging creatures ate through the underground wire, shutting down the system. Once there were 24 breaks detected, and it took the service person almost two hours to find and fix them all. I was glad we now had a solid fence. After the fiasco with Eva, I dared not try the Invisible Fence® with Zorra.

The trip to the island went smoothly. Bruce was coming out later, after work, and in the meantime, I decided to put up some flyers, especially in the supermarket where there was a community bulletin board. But first I needed to dose all the dogs with Frontline®, a flea and tick killer which is applied to the animal's back, between the shoulder blades. I should've done it two days earlier, to allow the solution to penetrate the fatty layer beneath the skin, but things got away from me, and I forgot.

Monkey and Argo accepted this treatment without a hassle. As entertainment for visitors, I had trained each of them to roll onto their backs, when I asked, "Who has a flea?" Not that either of them ever had fleas, unlike my poor Mercury. But this routine allowed me to check their undersides for ticks, which were prevalent on Shelter Island, due to the huge deer population. In fact, if a tick died, thanks to Frontline®, and its dehydrated body still was clinging to Monkey's belly, she'd lie on her back and look at me. This was her way of telling me to check her. Argo did the same. It didn't occur to me to be careful with Zorra.

I called her, and she came to me. But just as I was about to begin the application, she bolted. She darted across the lawn and flung herself under my car, which was parked in the driveway. Luckily, I had closed the front gates. She refused to come out. I lay on my stomach and spoke to her, showing her a biscuit held between my fingers. But she wouldn't budge. I reached towards her, and to my surprise, she bared her teeth. I remembered how long it took me to put the collar on her that first time, and I realized I couldn't remain on the ground, on the pebbly stones, much longer. I thought, then, if I gently prodded her from behind, with my telescoping feather duster, she might move out. Then I could leash her up and try again with the Frontline®. I went inside to the utility closet and fetched it. When I slid the duster towards her, again she showed teeth. Perhaps in her early days as a street dog, she had been abused with a stick or a bat. But I had to get her out so I could go to the store and put up the flyer. I exerted more pressure on the duster. She jumped, not realizing that under a car there's no room for such a move. She hit something. I heard a squeal, and then I watched as she rushed from her hiding place. Blood dripped from her lip. I felt terrible. Up until then, I had made good progress with her, and now I was afraid she would no longer trust me.

Zorra licked the blood until it stopped flowing. She had a small gash near her chin. Surprisingly, she let me approach her, but I didn't try to touch her. I invited her into the house. Monkey and Argo surrounded her, sniffing the unfamiliar scent of the wound. I went back to the car and brought in Zorra's blanket. I placed it on the floor, in a corner and she lay down. Then I went to the supermarket. I posted flyers in several other stores as well. I contacted ARF, the animal rescue fund of the Hamptons. They ran a big adoption program at their facility in East Hampton, and I offered to bring Zorra around from an "interview." She was such a beautiful dog, I was sure someone would want her.

My husband arrived that evening and he played with Zorra outside. She loved to retrieve tennis balls and Frisbees®. I told him I was taking her to ARF on Monday so they could assess her. I planned to stay on the island for the entire week to help her find a home.

That night, Bruce went to bed first, and when I came upstairs, Zorra was curled up next to him. She was used to sleeping with Ana, so naturally, she figured this was where she was supposed to spend the night. I didn't mind. Monkey already was in her spot on top of my pillow, and Argo was on his cushion under the bed. But Zorra hadn't left any room for me. I asked her to move over, and when she didn't, I gently nudged her. That's when she snapped at me. I was so surprised, in a reflex action I hit her. It wasn't a solid hit, just a flick of my hand, and I know it didn't hurt her, but immediately, I felt ashamed. I pride myself in never using physical force with any of my animals. I wondered if the incident under the car had made her wary. I hoped she wasn't afraid of me.

Ana and I had agreed that we would never place Zorra or Lucy in a shelter. They needed real homes. So, with this in mind, I drove to East Hampton and met with the woman who handled adoptions. I gave her some flyers, the ones with that terrific Central Park shot of Zorra, and I explained what I knew of Zorra's history. While I was filling out forms, an aide took Zorra to another area where they temperament tested the dogs. Zorra looked back at me as the young girl led her away.

No one on the list of adopters was looking for a dog like Zorra, but the woman said she would call me should that change. She told me Zorra was a nice dog. We drove back to the island. Deep inside I was glad there were no potential adopters at ARF. I was hoping Zorra could stay on the island, or find a great place in the city. Towards the end of the week, a woman called and said she had seen one of the flyers. Her children wanted a dog. I invited her to bring them to see Zorra. The boy was perhaps twelve, and the girl eleven, just the right age to romp with a frisky young dog. They lived on the island, on a quiet street, though the yard wasn't fenced. I wasn't keen about that. As I spoke with the woman, whose name I've forgotten, the children played with Zorra. It seemed a good fit.

We agreed that the family could take Zorra home for a day or two, and if all went well, they'd adopt her. I had explained that she wasn't my dog, and that the woman would have to sign an adoption agreement, which stated that if for any reason, they no longer wanted Zorra, no matter where they might live at the time, Ana or I would come and take her back. The agreement had to be notarized.

Two days later, I received a call from the woman. She was returning Zorra. Her son and his friends had been roughhousing in the yard. The daughter was playing with Zorra, and when one of the boys accidentally lurched towards them, Zorra, perceiving a threat, snapped at him. The woman apologized. She said her daughter loved Zorra, and cried when she left, but that they couldn't have a nippy dog with such big teeth in the house. I told her I understood.

No one else called to adopt Zorra. Summer on Shelter Island would begin in a few weeks, and I suggested to my husband, and to Ana, that

Zorra spend the summer with us. That way, I could keep training her and socializing her, and perhaps, find her a home. By then, I was sure that no one in the city was going to adopt her. Response to our flyers had been disappointing, and there had been no additional inquiries through PetFinder. Ana always had hoped that I would adopt Zorra. But adding a third dog was a big step. It meant no more "family" vacations in Puerto Rico because Zorra could never fit under the seat in the cabin, and I wouldn't ship her below. From my dog show days, I'd heard terrible stories of dogs arriving at their destinations, in their crates, dead. I made an agreement with Ana, though I didn't tell my husband about the plan just yet. If, during the course of the summer, Monkey and Argo accepted her, we would adopt Zorra.

Chapter 20

City Dog

Bruce drove to Shelter Island every Friday, arriving anytime between five o'clock in the afternoon and nine in the evening. His car, a BMW M5 wagon, imported from Europe, and made street legal to comply with U.S. regulations, had a special high performance engine that rumbled like an approaching earthquake. When he was three blocks away, Zorra knew he was near. She'd sit on the sofa in the sun porch, tall as a statue, and look towards the corner, her tail thumping a welcoming beat on the cushions. Within minutes, the sleek, black car pulled into the driveway. At that moment, I announced in a cheery voice, "It's your daddy," and all three dogs rushed to the door. As Bruce emerged from the car, I let everybody out. Zorra, ecstatic, jumped on him, while Monkey twirled around like a crazed top, and Argo peed on a shrub to welcome him, man to man.

With each successive weekend, my husband grew more and more fond of Zorra. Unlike the Schipperkes, who sought affection on their terms, Zorra was always eager for a pat, plus she loved to play. I had bought a soft Frisbee®, and Bruce spent a good part of the day tossing it for her to retrieve. In the sun, her black coat gleamed like a panther's as she charged up the hill to capture her toy. The first time I mentioned adopting her, Bruce made a face, but by the end of the summer, Zorra herself had convinced him. In September, she came back to the city with us.

Walking three dogs tested my skills. I always used Flexileads® with the Schipperkes. I wanted them to have the benefits of exercise plus a bit of freedom, but since they were Schipperkes, I never let them off lead until we were far from home, in the middle of the park. On lead, the Schips sometimes moved as though they were threading a May Pole, going under and around each other until the thin cord of the leash was braided. It wasn't that hard to undo when there were only two dogs, but with three, I pictured myself trussed like a turkey. I needn't have worried. Zorra walked by my side, slightly behind, never surging ahead like the Schipperkes. I used a standard six foot nylon lead with her, which was always slack in my hand. In time, as she became familiar with the park, I'd let her off. She never strayed very far.

Over the course of the summer, Zorra had proved she was house trained. She only peed once, on the porch rug, and that might've been because we came home late one night. But in the apartment, she developed bad behavior. She began urinating on the rug in the bedroom, always near the side of the bed where my husband slept. We weren't sure what to do. With the Schipperkes, I had used a crate for training, but Zorra was much larger, and our bedroom wouldn't accommodate a big crate. Besides, I knew she would freak out if confined. One weekend during the summer, my brother-in-law had visited us on Shelter Island. He'd brought a large crate he no longer needed. I figured I could acclimate Zorra, in case one day, I had to kennel her. I paved the way inside with treats, but as soon as Zorra neared the entrance, she shied away. After a few more tries, I stopped. Clearly, this was not a cozy den in her mind, but rather a trap of some kind, one to avoid at all costs. So, to save our rug, we bought hospital pads, not the wee-wee pads sold in pet stores which are treated with a scent that encourages dogs to "go." We didn't want Zorra to get the wrong message by enticing her with these "do-it-here" items. For almost a year, we put down the hospital pads. Sometimes, several days went by without her using them, making us think she was finished with peeing indoors. We'd take up the pads. Then she'd wet the rug again. Zorra was lucky she ended up with us. Other people might not have been so forgiving, and perhaps would have turned her in to a shelter. We decided that in time, we'd get a new rug.

Zorra had other surprises for us in addition to peeing on the rug. Often, when we came home after an evening out, we found shredded tissues scattered on the floor. Zorra liked to go into the waste paper baskets and pluck them out, leaving a trail as in *Hansel and Gretel*. Any handbag or tote left within her reach was also fair game. She especially enjoyed finding a lipstick or chapstick and ever so gently nibbling the top of the case or the cap in such a way that it couldn't be used again. We never caught her in the act, but we knew she was the culprit.

The apartment building in which we lived was owned by Mt. Sinai Hospital, and late in the summer, we had been informed that they had sold it to a developer. There were plans to renovate the 1929 building, upgrade the electrical and heating systems, then sell the units as condominiums. Many people in the building had lived there for decades, as had we, and many of the apartments were rent controlled or rent stabilized. We formed a tenants' committee to fight the conversion, but ultimately, a non-eviction plan was accepted, and the renovation began. The dogs, especially Zorra, didn't like all these strange workmen traipsing through the lobby, carrying scary looking things such as ladders and pails. I had to keep her leash short and tight, or she'd lunge at them with bared teeth.

Ana had decided to keep Lucy, so with that, the adoption campaign officially ended. We both agreed, that even if someone were to suddenly show up, offering to take one or both dogs, we'd say no. Zorra had become part of our family, yet in the hierarchy, she was last. My husband often grumbled, good-naturedly, that *he* was low dog in the pack because I gave all my attention to my canine buddies. I played with them, groomed them daily, and took them on long walks in the park. There was an order to the way I fed them, based on who had been the first dog in our household. It was Monkey, then Argo, then Zorra. Although she was much larger than the Schipperkes, she never tried to shove them out of the way to get at their dishes. I think she understood she was lucky to be where she was, and she always deferred to the little dogs. They ate twice a day, and sometimes Bruce fed them. Occasionally, he forgot the pecking order, and if I saw him put Zorra's dish down before Monkey's or Argo's, I'd give him a stern lecture on pack behavior.

Chapter 21

Dog Sitters and Travel

In February, my husband and I joined a group of people on a trip to Cambodia, organized through the Joyce Theatre in New York. Three years earlier, when we had gone to Cuba, we left the dogs with our friend Grace. But now we had three dogs, and I thought it was better for them to stay on Shelter Island where they could romp in their own yard.

I had found a dog sitter, a middle-aged man named Joseph. He was a large fellow, over six feet tall, and he drove an old pick-up truck which barely squeezed through our front gate. He was also an opera singer who wasn't engaged by any particular company at that time. So he stayed in people's homes and watched their pets or watered their plants. I decided to try him after checking a reference and hearing a good report. Our Shelter Island house is furnished with antiques and I pointed out to Joseph that he had to keep this in mind at all times. Old things break easier, and tables, with age-worn patinas, grow permanent rings from glasses or soda cans placed directly upon them. I showed him how to turn on an old lamp which sat on the sideboard in the dining room, and I explained about Argo's occasional bouts with dirty poopies. He seemed willing to take care of everything, including butt clean-up, during the three weeks we were gone.

The Cambodia trip actually started in Bangkok, at the Mandarin Oriental Hotel, where all the travelers in our small group of sixteen met and spent a few days getting over jet lag, going to the spa, and seeing the sights. Bruce and I had left a few days earlier and stopped in Hong Kong for a couple of days. This was our first trip to Southeast Asia.

It coincided with the Lunar New Year, a time of lion dances and great festivity for Chinese families. From our hotel window, we watched the spectacular fireworks color the sky over Kowloon Harbor. I had thought spending sixteen hours on a plane, traveling through multiple time zones and crossing the International Date Line would knock me flat, but with a couple of well-timed naps, both Bruce and I hopped right into exploring the city. Shopping, though, proved a disappointment. Most stores were closed. We hadn't realized how much of a family holiday this was. Luckily, the restaurants in the big hotels were open, though we would have preferred dining at typical places, many of which also were closed for the New Year.

We flew to Bangkok, and although February back home often brings hefty snowstorms, February in this city was summery. I thought about the dogs. I was glad I'd left them on Shelter Island. If New York got hit with more snow, after the late January blast that had deposited a record 20 inches, at least I wouldn't have to worry about their safety. We had a fellow who plowed the driveway, and as long as Joseph kept the gates closed, and checked the fences to make sure deer hadn't knocked them down, Monkey, Argo and Zorra could enjoy carefree romps. Bruce assured me the dogs were fine, and I guess I knew that, but after what had happened to Mercury, I never could feel one hundred percent at ease.

Although a few people in our group had a dog at home, no one had three, and no one, except the couple who had been on our Cuba trip, had ever heard of Schipperkes. My husband always carried a photo of Monkey and Argo in his wallet, and I had one tucked into my passport case. It was a great conversation opener when someone asked, "Do you have children?" One of us would reply, "No, we have Schipperkes." Then out came the photo. In time, as we socialized with the others, over dinner or drinks, I spoke about how I had showed Argo myself at Westminster. Sometimes, I mentioned the book I'd written about the breed. But I seldom shared the story of Mercury. Even dog lovers' eyes would glaze over if I hit them with that sad tale.

Despite the heat, Bangkok delighted us. For the two days we were there, we saw everything from the floating markets to the Grand Palace, which included the Temple of the Emerald Buddha, one of Thailand's holiest sites. It astounded me then, as it did on subsequent trips to Southeast Asia, that hundreds, if not thousands, of diamonds, rubies, emeralds and sapphires adorned these unguarded statues and nobody stole them.

We then flew to Siem Reap in Cambodia, the base camp for exploring the magnificent temples of Angkor. We stayed at the Grand Hotel d'Angkor, which thrilled me, because this was where Jackie Kennedy had stayed when she visited the ruins in the 1960s. My husband found thrills of a different nature, namely the local beers, plus tolerant attitudes towards cigar smoking. Like a truffle-snorting pig, he could find a cold brew no matter where we were in our explorations. On our air conditioned bus, traveling to and from the sites, people got used to hearing the pop of a can. They'd chuckle among themselves and someone would say, "There goes Bruce."

Since this was a Joyce affiliated trip, we saw several Cambodian dance programs, both at the hotel and at outside venues. The dancers were sewn into their elaborate costumes by hand, which meant no beer or tea drinking once the last stitch was tied off. I told Bruce he could never join a Cambodian troupe. He definitely had the wrong body type, plus he couldn't last more than a few hours without a beer.

I spent my birthday exploring Angkor Wat with our group and a local guide, a fellow who spoke excellent English and who had encyclopedic knowledge of every bas-relief on the temple walls. The site is so vast, and the history so detailed, that after a while a few of us wished we could sneak away and sit down under a banyan tree, joining my hooky-playing, cigar-puffing husband for a cold one.

We visited all the requisite sights, including the odoriferous Tonle Sap Lake. Never have I smelled anything so vile, a combination of rotting fish, dung, animals, and fouled water. Yet people lived on this lake, washed their clothes in it, drank from it, used it as a toilet, and still somehow survived. We took a boat ride on the lake, past a floating village of stilt houses observing farm animals such as pigs living alongside these dwellings on rafts, which formed a type of back yard. As our boat's propeller churned the latte-colored water, I made sure to sit away from the rail. I didn't want one drop of it to land on my skin.

We moved on to Phnom Penh, and while there, we heard that the weather in New York continued cold, and that there had been a bit more snow, but not a major storm. I hoped Joseph remembered to wipe the dogs' feet after they were out in the yard. At home, I slathered their paws with Musher's Secret®, a thick, greasy product, originally used for sled dogs, that prevents snow and ice from balling between the toes. I didn't ask Joseph to use it on Monkey, Argo, and Zorra. If he weren't thorough about cleaning it off once inside the house, I'd have greasy paw prints all over the sofa.

This was the first year I'd missed Westminster in as long as I can remember, but I couldn't complain. The trip had been everything I had imagined, exotic, fascinating, filled with good food, wine, and, for the most part, congenial travel mates, including my husband. Phnom

Penh, however, was interesting in a different way. It was here that the Khmer Rouge depopulated the city by sending its inhabitants to the countryside for forced labor. Intellectuals, identified as people who wore glasses, were tortured and shot. I can still picture the grim "Museum of Crime," the Toul Sleng Genocide Museum, which was once a high school, and then a prison and interrogation facility. Guidebooks state that this prison processed over 17,000 people, seven of whom survived. Piles of human skulls, stacked one upon the other, behind a glass wall bear testament to the horror that befell these Cambodians.

We saw a few more "wats" or temples, and then returned to Bangkok for two and a half more days of sightseeing and shopping.

Both Bruce and I had fallen in love with this part of the world, and we decided to return, perhaps the following year. But at that moment, we were ready to go home. I hadn't called Joseph while we were gone, though I'd given him our itinerary and contact information. I was operating under that old saying, "no news is good news."

After we landed at JFK, we picked up the car and drove back into the city. I was anxious to get the dogs, but with our luggage, there wouldn't have been room for the Schipperkes' crates, nor enough space for Zorra to lounge on the back seat. As soon as I entered the apartment, I called Joseph. Everything was fine, he said, and I told him we were coming out the next morning to get the dogs and probably stay overnight. In anticipation of jet lag, Bruce had taken off the remaining two days of the week.

About a foot of snow still was on the ground, but our caretaker had done an excellent job of clearing the driveway. All three dogs flew out of the house, the moment we arrived, followed by Joseph. Some studies have reported that dogs have no sense of time, but the way these pooches greeted us, it looked as though they thought we'd been away for years. Monk twirled, Zorra jumped, and Argo appeared to chase his non-existent tail. And that's when I saw a large turd, the size of a golf ball, stuck, or perhaps frozen, to his behind. Joseph and my husband were exchanging pleasantries and chatting about the trip. I interrupted.

"Joseph, look at this poor dog," I said. "I thought you were going to take care of him."

"Oh, I didn't notice," he replied. "I'm sorry."

I had a snide answer ready to shoot from my lips, but I didn't say anything. I realized I might have to use his services again. With our new love for Southeast Asia, Bruce and I needed someone willing to stay on Shelter Island with three dogs in the dead of winter, when restaurants are closed, and any resident who can afford to, has gone down to Florida or the islands. But I was pissed. How could Joseph not have seen Argo running around with what amounted to a giant suppository extending from his butt?

Once inside, Joseph told us he had had a few mishaps. The lamp, which I had so carefully shown him how to use, now was minus its pull chain. He was supposed to have turned it on with the light switch and not touched the lamp itself, but he'd forgotten. The chain broke. Then he tried to fix it, and the lamp base came apart. Upstairs, he had had a small collision with the glass shelf that extended from the medicine chest towards the toilet. Because he was so large, when he stood up after using the facility, his shoulder caught the edge of the shelf and it crashed to the floor. I assured him it was all right, and that we easily could replace the shelf, though internally, I was seething. "What a clumsy oaf," I would have said, if I weren't thinking ahead to next year's trip and the need for a dog sitter. But then Joseph made one more confession. He said one day he'd gone off to the supermarket, and instead of leaving Zorra in the house with Monkey and Argo, he'd put her in the cottage. She panicked and chewed through a section of the sliding wood door, a door we had recently replaced at a hefty cost. At that moment, though I didn't say anything, I knew we'd have to find another dog sitter.

We returned to the city the next day. During our absence, the construction crew had put in risers for the heating system upgrade. Unfortunately for us, these ran through our hall closet, eating up half the space. Our bookcase in the small back room had been demolished as had the one in the living room, to accommodate the pipes. The risers, though covered with sheet rock and painted to blend in with our walls, had diminished the size of our rooms. My closet, too, had shrunk by one third. Before we left on the trip, the project manager had provided storage for our clothes in one of the empty apartments. Now, he told us, that apartment was scheduled for renovation, so we needed to retrieve our garments. There was no room to put anything. I bought a coat rack and placed it in my bathtub, hanging the clothes, displaced from my closet, on its metal bar. From that day on, I had no choice but to take showers in Bruce's bathroom.

Chapter 22

Night Walk

Zorra continued to pee on the hospital pads. Spring came, and along with it the start of our New York City Ballet subscription. On May 12th, we headed out to the ballet, stopping at Gabriel's restaurant on West 60th Street for our usual pre-theatre dinner. Sometimes, and especially if I'd played tennis during the day, the wine we drank at dinner made me sleepy. It had the same effect on my husband, who was still working, and had to drive in from New Jersey, often amidst heavy traffic. Frequently, one or both of use fell asleep during the performance. We blamed outside influences, fresh air, alcohol, and stress, refusing to consider that perhaps we were growing old. City Ballet normally offers three ballets during the course of an evening, with two intermissions. That night, we decided to leave during the second one since we had seen the third offering several times in past seasons. We returned home a little after 9 o'clock. I said I'd take out the dogs.

I took them across the street, into the park, on the path above Fifth Avenue. This was our usual route. It was a pleasant evening, and I decided to walk a bit further, towards the East Meadow, past the playground. Above the treetops, across the field, lights twinkled from the co-ops on the West Side. It was quiet and magical, and I thought how lucky we were to be able to enjoy this park at night, as opposed to the old days, when sane people shunned it even in the daytime, because of drug addicts, muggers and crazed homeless people. Even so, my husband often worried if I didn't return within fifteen minutes. I turned around and told the dogs we had to go home. Monkey and Argo trotted sixteen feet ahead of me, the full extension of their Flexileads®. Zorra, on her shorter leash, stayed by my side. Suddenly, in the dim light of the vapor lamp, I saw a hulking shape standing alone on the path. It was a Rottweiler. Instinctively, I yanked back on the Schipperkes' leads, but it was too late. I heard a growl, then a yip. I dropped Argo's lead and saw him fall down the embankment. I rushed forward and in that second, the beast set upon Monkey. I let go of Zorra. Using the hard plastic handle of the Flexilead®, I beat the Rottweiler on its head and in its stomach. It stood there, motionless, as I screamed for help. My Monkey lay on the ground. Even in the murky light, I could see dark patches of blood. I kept hitting the Rottweiler and screaming. A man came up the steps. He was a slim black man, with light colored skin, dressed in a tropical shirt and tailored slacks. I noticed this because he was too well-dressed for the neighborhood. I also noticed the Rottweiler was wearing a harness, but no tags.

He said, "Miss, you better stop hitting that dog. He could turn on you."

I was on my knees, bent over Monkey. I looked up at him. "Is this your dog?" I said.

"No." With that, he disappeared into the night.

By then, police had arrived along with an ambulance. Someone had called 911. People had come out of their buildings and were gathered on the sidewalk across from the park. No one was sure what had happened. I wrapped Monkey in my raincoat and walked towards the crowd. Argo lay somewhere in the bushes, but I didn't look for him. I don't know why. I was sleepwalking in a nightmare. I didn't cry. I felt numb. Bruce appeared and I quickly told him what happened. He asked about Argo and I pointed to the park. A police officer told him not to go in there, but like the hero he was on 9/11, he did what he had to do. One of our neighbors had taken Zorra inside. Apparently, she'd run across Fifth Avenue to our building when the attack began. Luckily, there was no traffic that night. I borrowed $20 from another neighbor and jumped in a cab with Monkey. I told the driver to rush us to the Animal Medical Center, the very place where Mercury had been taken after his terrible accident. I begged the driver to run the lights when there were no other cars around. I knew Monkey was dying and every second counted. But he was a law abiding citizen. Who knows if it would have made any difference? When we arrived at the Medical Center, I raced up the ramp, screaming "emergency." A veterinarian appeared and showed me into a room with a steel examination table. I explained what had happened as I lay Monkey down. It was then that I noticed the damage. The Rottweiler had bitten through her underside. A strand of intestine, pale and shiny as mother-of-pearl, protruded from the hole in her belly.

She was dead, but somehow I still couldn't cry. I suppose I was in shock. The veterinarian offered condolences. I mumbled a "thank you." I put on my raincoat. It was stained with blood. An attendant put Monkey's body in a cardboard box, taped it up, and handed it to me. Slowly, I walked down the ramp and left the building. There was a gas station on the corner, and I didn't see any cabs. I saw two men in an SUV at one of the pumps. They looked like the kind of guys who might play thugs or drug dealers in a movie, but I approached them anyway.

"Are you going uptown? Can you give me a lift?" I said. "My dog just got killed. I need to get home."

I don't quite remember if they answered me or ignored me. Maybe my blood stained coat turned them off. Just then, a taxi rounded the corner. I hailed it and got in. It wasn't possible that Miss Monkey was in the box on my lap, dead.

The doorman told me my husband had found Argo and had taken him to the Animal Medical Center in his car, which had been parked near our building. He told me the police had taken the Rottweiler away, and that the animal didn't put up a fight or try to run. He said how sorry he was that such a terrible thing had happened. His eyes shimmered, but he managed to hold back the tears. I went upstairs and placed Monkey's box in the kitchen. Shortly afterwards, Bruce came home. Argo had been standing on his own when he found him. Bruce tried to pick him up, but the dog bit him. Clearly the animal was in pain. Bruce grabbed the lead and led Argo to the car, and somehow the dog hopped in.

The veterinarian's initial assessment gave us hope. He thought the wounds looked treatable. But they would have to open him up to check for further damage. After surgery, we could get a more accurate prognosis. Someone would call us in a few hours. Bruce had been crying non-stop, yet I was still in a zombie-like state, unable to tap into any kind of emotion. Perhaps, subconsciously, I thought that crying was accepting that Monkey was gone, and my mind wasn't ready to do that.

Zorra shied away from me and showed teeth when I tried to remove her collar. I realized she was frightened so I spoke softly to her, but left her alone. I was thankful she had the smarts to save herself from the Rottweiler by running home.

The veterinarian called at 3 a.m. with bad news. Surgery revealed that all of Argo's organs had been punctured. It was unlikely they could save him. Even with the slimmest chance, I was not going to put Argo through a lengthy and probably futile rehabilitation. I had learned my lesson with Mercury. I took Bruce's car and drove to the animal hospital. I'd brought Argo's favorite blanket, and I wrapped him in it, while the veterinarian administered the needle that ended his life. He, too, was placed in a cardboard box. By the time I returned home, Bruce had cleared the shelves in the refrigerator, creating enough space to hold both Monkey and Argo.

The next morning, Friday, we drove to Shelter Island. During the night, when it had been impossible to sleep, I had emailed *The New York Post* and described the savage attack on the Schipperkes. Just before we left for the island, the reporter had called and interviewed me by phone. The story ran on Saturday, under the headline "Dogs in Park Horror."

Bruce dug a grave and we buried the dogs, on the little hill where Mercury rested. When we arrived at the house, I had opened the boxes in order to place some of their favorite things inside. Argo crossed the rainbow bridge with his muskrat coat, and Monkey had her soccer ball and squeaky toy. Suddenly, the finality hit me. I sat down in the dirt and cried.

Inside, Zorra lay on her bed and kept her distance. I feared she thought I'd been hitting Monkey when I had crouched on the ground and pummeled the Rottweiler. There was no way I could explain to her what had happened. I hoped it wouldn't diminish her trust in me. I had worked so hard during the past year to build her confidence.

We returned to the city on Sunday. The answering machine brimmed with messages from reporters and a few television stations asking for interviews. I didn't return the calls. We were old news by then, and besides, who needed to listen to the usual inanities such as, "That must've been horrible. How do you feel?"

A sergeant from the Central Park Precinct, an animal lover, heard what had happened and decided to get involved. Although he was not one of the police officers who'd responded to the 911 call that evening, he phoned and left a message on my machine with startling news. The Rottweiler, Max, had been adopted out through the Animal Control facility on East 110th Street. He'd been microchipped to someone who lived in the Bronx. When I called Animal Control the next day, a representative said this person told them he'd given the dog away a year ago. Of course, they wouldn't give me the name. I had no way of finding out who had the dog in the park that night, short of hiring a private detective.

On Wednesday, my husband and I walked down to the 23rd Precinct on East 102nd Street to see if a police report had been filed. This was the precinct that had sent five squad cars in response to the 911 call. Two young women, perhaps in their late teens were in the lobby, waiting, I'm not sure for what. I struck up a conversation with them while my husband approached the officer at the desk. I told the girls how a Rottweiler had killed my two dogs.

"What was his name?" one of the young women asked.

"Who?" I wondered why she'd want to know the name of one of my dogs.

"The Rottweiler," she said.

"Oh. Max."

"My god," she said, "that's my brother's dog."

She told me her brother had been visiting her. She lived near the northwestern corner of Central Park. He'd brought Max, a dog someone had given him just a week earlier. He went into the park that Thursday night, walking Max on a chain lead and a harness. The leash had opened and Max had gotten away. She asked me what was going to happen.

"They'll kill him," I said.

She recoiled, thinking I meant her brother. "Travis?"

"No, Max."

Her brother's name was Travis Jackson and he lived in Queens. But right now, she told me, he was in Jamaica. He undoubtedly had left town right after the incident. I was sure he was the man I'd seen in the park. Over the next few days, I looked up every Travis Jackson I could find, but I couldn't come up with a phone number that matched an address in Queens. And my husband couldn't come up with a police report. The officer had explained that they didn't file reports when it came to animals, only if a human got hurt. On the slow walk back to our apartment, I told my husband what I'd learned from the young woman. We both felt that her story about the leash opening was a lie.

Well-meaning people told me to sue, and at first that seemed like a good idea. I was angry. My dogs were dead. Someone should pay. But who? Travis Jackson? Animal Control? The most I could've recouped was the purchase price of the dogs. Under New York law, beloved pets are considered property, like a table or chair. There is no compensation for pain and suffering. It was no surprise, then, that the few lawyers I contacted through connections on my Internet dog lists, showed no interest in the case.

The sergeant had promised that the Rottweiler would never leave the Animal Control facility alive. He had given me Max's intake number as well as his own direct phone line so that I could check on the dog's status and report back to him. When I called Animal Control a week later, I learned that Max had been euthanized. I was sure he had been a trained fighting dog, one programmed to kill other animals, but to never attack a human. Otherwise, he could have easily torn me to shreds. It had been after nine o'clock when this happened, and in those days, the Parks Department offered an off-leash courtesy to dog owners, which has now become official policy. From nine o'clock at night until one a.m. when the park officially closes, then from when it opens in the morning until nine, dogs are allowed off-lead in Central Park. I'd always thought this was insane. The thought of loose dogs roaming in the dark always made me a bit nervous. That's why I kept to the path across from our building. Few people used it at night. But now I was incensed. An off-lead dog had killed my beloved pets. I felt it was time to curtail these freedoms and change the courtesy to the daylight hours, from dawn to 9 a.m.

I wrote to Mayor Bloomberg, telling him what had happened to Monkey and Argo, and urging him to speak to the Parks Commissioner about restricting the off-lead hours. He and Bruce had been fraternity brothers at Johns Hopkins, so I anticipated a personal note. Nine months later, I received a letter, written by an aide, telling me the mayor was sorry about what had happened to our dogs. There was no mention of changing the off-lead hours.

Monkey and Argo had been well-known in the neighborhood and the story of their deaths had made its way onto several dog lists on the Internet. Sympathy cards arrived from all over the country and neighbors sent flowers. Each time I opened a card, my eyes teared, as did my husband's. Zorra missed her little pals and she continued to pee in the bedroom. We kept buying hospital pads. I took up Monkey and Argo's dishes and put them in the cupboard. It was too sad to see them there, empty, and to watch Zorra sniff around them, perhaps wondering if somehow, just maybe, one or both of the Schips might suddenly barge into the kitchen and growl at her.

Chapter 23

Marlena

Zorra and I continued to take our morning walk in the park. It felt strange not having Monkey and Argo tugging on their Flexileads®, surging ahead of me. People who knew what had happened expressed their condolences when they saw us. Others, noticing I had but one dog, asked the whereabouts of Monkey and Argo. When I told them, many ungraciously pressed me for details. Almost everyone asked where the Rottweiler's owner had been, and when I said the dog was alone, they'd ask, "You mean there wasn't any owner?" Others asked if I'd gotten the name of the man who'd appeared in the park. At first, I was passive and said, no. Eventually, I lost patience and asked them if they'd just seen their dog bitten in half by a Rottweiler, would they have thought to ask the guy's name? For the next month, until it was time to go to Shelter Island for the summer, I had to relive that horrible night as people who'd been out of town or hadn't seen me in a while posed the question, "Only one dog?"

Both Bruce and I agreed we needed another Schipperke. We loved Zorra, but she wasn't used to being an "only child," and we missed not having a little black fox around the house. I decided to put out a call for an older, mellow Schipperke. At that point, I didn't have the mental energy to deal with a puppy or a young dog that needed training. Through the Internet, I contacted members of the Schipperke Club of America, most of whom knew what had happened. I was lucky. Ruth Bucy, a breeder in Colorado, was downsizing her kennel. She had an eight year-old spayed female for sale. Her name was Marlena, and she had just celebrated her birthday on May 9th, the day after Monkey had turned eleven. She was a champion, now retired, and her full name was Champion Coda's Torchsong Trilogy. One of Ruth's friends, who had shown Marlena to her championship, emailed me a show shot of her. She was beautiful, but even if she'd had warts on her nose, I would've bought her. Our hearts cried out for a Schipperke.

In early June, Marlena flew in from Denver, and I went to Newark Airport to pick her up. Like a nervous mother, I arrived too far in advance, and spent my time pacing around the small area that Continental Airlines provided for pet shipping and pick-up. As a show dog, Marlena was a seasoned traveler, but she never had flown so far on her own. Finally her crate appeared. I looked through the grate and saw a pair of dark eyes watching me. I opened the door and affixed the short slip lead I'd brought. Marlena stepped out. She seemed bewildered. I scratched her behind the ears. Then I signed the release papers and picked up the crate. The two of us walked outside to the car, to our new life together.

New York City is a lot noisier than Eton, Colorado, where Marlena had lived. I worried that she might feel overwhelmed. And then there was Zorra. Would the big dog make the newcomer nervous? These thoughts rumbled around in my mind as I drove towards the city. Ruth had told me that Marlena and another bitch in her kennel were not getting along. They often fought, and Marlena was dominant. Luckily, Zorra was gentle. There had never been any issues with Monkey, so I hoped there wouldn't be any now.

I would have liked to have introduced the "girls" on neutral ground, the way every article and book on dogs advises, but that was impractical, so I had asked Ana if she could keep Zorra for me that afternoon. This would give Marlena a chance to inspect her new home. Later, on his way back from work, Bruce could stop by and pick up Zorra. For several days, I had told Zorra that Marlena was coming, just as we had primed Monkey for her "puppy," Argo. This time I used the word "friend."

When Zorra arrived later that evening, the two dogs sniffed each other, and that was it. Neither raised a scruff or growled. In fact, Marlena had made no sound from the moment I'd retrieved her from the airport. Her silence continued for months, and I thought, perhaps, she had been debarked. But then, one day, on Shelter Island, she joined Zorra in a chorus announcing a visitor. Up until then, I surmised, she hadn't been convinced that her new home truly was hers to defend.

The summer unfolded lazily, with the usual Shelter Island events plugged into our calendar weeks in advance. In mid-July, I took Zorra and Marlena to the blessing of the animals at the Catholic Church. Marlena won a ribbon for being the smallest dog. Luckily, that year, no children had shown up with Chihuahuas, Toy Poodles, or puppies. Though this prize wasn't as prestigious as going Best of Breed, it showed that my girl still was in the ribbons.

Marlena's personality revealed itself slowly. Like Zorra, she had a few surprises up her furry sleeve as well. One afternoon, before we had left for Shelter Island for the summer, I'd come home to find one of my shoes in the living room. It was the mate of a brand new pair I had just bought for $250. The toe cap was black patent leather, a shiny temptation, I suppose for this shoe fetishist Schipperke. I picked up the shoe. Marlena had peeled the patent leather from its canvas backing. I thought for a moment that perhaps Zorra had done it, so carefully had the slicing been executed. But later that week, while Bruce and I were reading newspapers in the living room, Marlena came running in with one of his loafers in her mouth. This was an amazing feat for a little Schipperke since the shoe was bigger than her head. "Bad girl," I shouted. Marlena dropped the shoe and gave me a look that said, "I may be bad, but I'm awfully cute." From then on, my husband and I made sure to keep our shoes in our closets with the doors securely closed.

Chapter 24

Mozart

We all returned to the city after Labor Day, and the next month, I received a call from a woman at Central Park Paws, an organization that provides information and sponsors activities for dog owners. A woman named Karen had called and asked if Paws could help her find a home for her Schipperke. She was moving to the west coast, to a job that required extensive travel, and she wanted to avoid upsetting the Schip by putting him in a kennel or hiring dog sitters to take care of him while she was gone. He was ten years old and his name was Mozart. She had adopted him from a shelter when he was five.

The Paws woman, whose name I've forgotten, immediately thought of me. She didn't know that Marlena had joined our household. I reassured her. "We were three before, we can be three again."

I asked for Karen's phone number. On a warm fall Sunday, I walked across the park to the West Side, to an address where she and I had agreed to meet. I waited in front, on the sidewalk for a good fifteen minutes. Finally, when I looked down the street, I saw them. A Schipperke's silhouette and gait are quite distinctive, and even from a distance, any person familiar with the breed can spot them. "This is Mozart," Karen said.

She gave me a plastic bag that contained some dog food. "He eats anything."

She handed me the leash, turned around and headed back down the street. From the way her shoulders heaved, I knew she was crying. Mozart watched her. He was wearing a collar and I was afraid he'd slip out of it if he tried to chase after his "mom." I always use harnesses on my Schipperkes. For one, harnesses didn't press on their throats, which, in some lines, are prone to collapsing tracheas. Plus, harnesses are safer. The dog can't duck out of them. I picked up Mozart and carried him into the park. The moment I put him down, he saw a squirrel. He lunged towards it, and after that, he never looked back.

Compared to Marlena, Mozart was a poor physical specimen. He was skinny, with spindly legs, and his back, instead of being level or sloping slightly downward, had a hump, like a camel's. His head was what breeder's call "snipey," too pointy and vulpine. I was sure he he'd been born in a puppy mill.

As we approached the East Side, I called Bruce. I had instructed him to take Zorra out of the apartment. I planned to meet them in the park, on neutral territory, just the way the dog books recommended. Marlena remained at home. I wasn't worried about her. She was even tempered and got along with everyone. When Zorra saw me approach with Mozart, she wagged her tail. Then, she sniffed him, and he took a whiff of her. No one challenged the other. I smiled at my husband. "I think we're good."

Karen hadn't given me Mozart's bed or anything other than the small amount of food. She'd explained, somewhat sheepishly, that she'd had some problems with her partner and had been forced to leave their apartment in a hurry. She was planning to move to L.A., but this turn of events intensified the need to quickly find a good home for her dog. I told her not to worry. I'd buy Mozart a new bed and anything else his little Schipperke heart desired. Mozart didn't know it at the time, but like Marlena and Zorra, this little fox had found Nirvana.

Chapter 25

Marlena Takes a Hike

A few weeks after Mozart arrived, I found a lump on Marlena's belly. It was round and hard, like a marble. She'd been lying on her back, the way Monkey and Argo did, waiting for someone to scratch her. I didn't even have to ask, "Who has a flea?" I called my veterinarian and he told me to bring her in. The lump had to be removed and biopsied. My heart sank. What if Marlena had cancer? What if she were going to die? After losing Monkey and Argo, the possibility filled me with sadness. I knew Bruce was worried as well. Over dinner one night, I started to ask, "What happens if she . . ."

"Don't even think like that," he said.

Marlena's surgery was successful and the lump proved benign. She was a strong little bitch and recuperated quickly. When the stitches came out, an observer never would have known she had had an operation, except for a missing nipple which had been removed by the scalpel.

I was walking three dogs again. Both Mozart and Marlena fit the red, black and tan Burberry plaid harnesses Monkey and Argo had worn. But instead of Flexileads®, I used regular nylon leashes. Never again would I let my dogs get sixteen feet ahead of me, especially at night. Then, a few weeks later, while I was giving Marlena a tummy rub, I found more lumps. They were small, more bumps, than true lumps, but I knew I had to take her back to the veterinarian. He was as surprised as I. There had been no sign of any abnormalities after the last surgery.

Once again, Marlena recuperated quickly, but the vet didn't want to send her home right away. He thought it best to watch her for a few days, in case new bumps sprouted. She spent the weekend, plus Monday in his little animal hospital in the basement of the practice. He said I could visit her, which I did. When I opened the door of her crate, she stood and put her paw on my shoulder. I told her she'd come home soon.

Bruce left work early on Tuesday so he could meet me at the veterinarian and give Marlena a ride home. A cloth bandage encircled her body, holding in place the gauze and antibiotic ointment that had been applied to the stitches. To a casual observer, it looked as though she was wearing a trendy t-shirt. Carefully, I carried her to the car. Marlena didn't act as though she'd just had surgery. The moment we entered the apartment, she zoomed to her dish, and, finding it empty, quickly checked Mozart's and Zorra's. I could see she was disappointed, so I gave her a welcome home treat.

That night, Bruce agreed to walk Mozart and Zorra. I took Marlena. Because of her stitches, I chose not to put the harness on her. I opted for a leather slip collar that I had used at dog shows after finishing in the ring. Outside, across from our building, Mozart peed on a tree. Marlena and I were a few feet away. She squatted. "Good girl, pee-pee here," I said.

But in the very next second, she lunged forward. The leash opened, and like a rocket, Marlena flew across Fifth Avenue.

The leash dangled in my hand like a dead eel. I screamed, "Marlena!" Apparently, she had seen something, a rat or a squirrel, rummaging in front of the hospital and her hunting instincts kicked in. My husband rushed over. "Quick. Give me Mozart," I said. I tucked him under my arm like a football, hoping that Marlena might see him and stop her crazed flight down the street. I dodged through the traffic and made it to the other side. "Steak. Chicken. Car ride." I threw a menu of enticing words into the night, but the little Schip kept going. I realized I couldn't catch her. She had turned the corner at 98th Street and disappeared. A young man pointed down the street when I asked, to no one in particular, if anyone had seen a loose dog run by. But most people were yakking on cell phones or trying to get a cab, too absorbed in their own worlds to have noticed a little black dog, wrapped in bandages, practically skittering across their feet.

I scratched Mozart under the chin. I felt numb. *The leash opened. The dog got away.* Travis Jackson's sister's words echoed in my mind. I put Mozart down on the sidewalk, then turned around and hurried home. Bruce was standing in front of our building with Zorra. From the arch in his brow, I knew he didn't fully understand what had happened. I explained as we hustled the dogs upstairs. That week, we had both our cars in the city. This enabled us to spread out and cover more territory as we searched for Marlena.

On the east side of Madison Avenue, beginning at 99th Street, housing projects stretched for half-mile uptown. Aside from Chihuahuas, who usually stayed on lead close to their owners, the dogs of choice there were Pit Bulls and Rottweilers. Often, they were loose. I opened my windows and cruised by, shouting, "Marlayyynnnnaaaa." It was after ten o'clock, and by this time most families were indoors, and it was still too early for restless young men and drug dealers to appear. When I reached 106th Street, I spotted my husband. I flashed my lights, and he noticed me. Hmm, I thought, things were improving, recalling the time he drove right by me as I stood on the sidewalk flailing my arms. I told him I had a plan.

We went back to the apartment and I booted up my computer. I found a photo of Monkey and quickly designed a flyer with our phone number and the offer of a reward. I printed fifty copies, grabbed tape and scissors and started towards the door. Zorra wagged her tail and trundled down the hallway, anticipating another walk, but it was Mozart who was chosen to come with us. I figured a live example of the kind of dog we were looking for might help us find Marlena.

The leash opened. The dog got away. Never in all my years of owning dogs had this happened. I hadn't thought it possible. We stopped by the police station, where I had met Travis Jackson's sister. I asked the community liaison officer if she would take a flyer and urge her colleagues to keep an eye out for my dog when they left for patrol. We papered lampposts along Madison Avenue, all the way up to 125th Street. We snaked through deserted side streets of once-elegant brownstones, still charming by day, but now eerily dark. A group of six young men, wearing hooded sweatshirts and low-riding hip hop jeans, glowered as we approached the corner they'd claimed as their own. It was close to midnight, and my guess is that they thought we were plainclothes cops or customers looking for drugs. I took a flyer and stepped out of the car.

"Excuse me, gentlemen, have you seen a dog like this?" I smiled as I handed a sheet to one of the guys. Normally, pictures of babies and animals make even the hardest person react with good cheer, but this fellow's lips remained firm. "She ran away tonight," I said. "If you see her, would you please call me?"

We cruised east to Lexington Avenue, then back up to Madison. My eyes darted from side to side, like a wary animal, searching for anything that moved. By one o'clock, we'd run out of supplies as well as people to approach. This was Wednesday morning, so there wasn't much street activity. In a way that was good. In this part on town on the weekends, gunfire often exploded. We returned home. My husband slept, but I couldn't. My eyes burned. My head hurt. I emailed the *New York Post* reporter who had written the story about Monkey and Argo. He never replied. Unless Marlena's escape ended tragically, there wasn't enough "meat" for tabloid coverage. I churned out more flyers. Dawn streaked through the window. I looked at my watch. In another two hours, the animal shelter opened. I planned to be first in line.

It was a clear, mild morning, more like Indian summer than mid November. In many ways it reminded me of September 11th, with a sky so blue, it almost seemed fake. So much had happened since then with regard to dogs. Ana and I had found Eva a home, Lucy and Zorra were settled, Monkey and Argo had died, and Mozart and Marlena had joined our household. Yet here I was again, in zombieland, feeling that none of this was real, that my beautiful Marlena couldn't possibly have run off into the night, bandaged and stitched, through city streets humming with traffic, and survived. I prayed that an animal control agent had picked her up and that, in a few moments, we'd be reunited.

The Center for Animal Care and Control on East 110th Street used to be the last stop for strays, a place where euthanization, not adoption, was the rule. Over time, thanks to an enlightened city government, the shelter became no-kill, meaning that any cat or dog that could possibly be adopted, would be given that chance. I had been to this facility once before, years ago, when I accompanied a friend who had to put down her dog. I remember the Pit Bulls brought in that day, scarred, tortured animals, some appearing to have been burned with cigarettes. It sickened me. How could anybody, even the worst thug, behave so cruelly towards an animal?

The woman at the front desk took my contact information and a flyer. I told her Marlena was wearing a collar without identification tags but that she was microchipped. The woman studied the flyer. She had never heard of a Schipperke. She asked me if I wanted a "walk through," a journey past crated dogs waiting for owners who might or might not ever come to fetch them. She said it was possible my dog had been picked up but not yet processed into the system. To this day, I can see the sad-eyed dogs sitting in cages, dispirited and lonely, hoping that each passing human might offer them love. I saw dogs both big and small. One or two looked purebred—a German Shepherd Dog and a Toy Poodle. Had their owners died without leaving instructions in their wills for the care of their pets? Or had they been abandoned, perhaps because someone moved to a "no dogs allowed" building, or because they'd become old and therefore required more and costly veterinary care? My eyes filled with tears as I glanced into their cages. Poor, dear sweet dogs, I thought. I was sure most of these animals would never get adopted.

Marlena wasn't there. I thanked the woman at the desk and said I'd call later, then stop by around four in the afternoon. Dogs and cats kept coming in all day, and if Marlena were loose on city streets, there was a good chance she'd get captured. As I walked home, the faces of the dogs in those cages haunted me. I knew they were going to die. No-kill doesn't mean they'll live confined forever, and, in my opinion, that's preferable. It is far more cruel to keep a dog for weeks, maybe months, in a cage or crate, with only limited exercise and interaction with people, than to give it a peaceful death. Sanctuaries like Best Friends are the exception. There, animals have outdoor space and lots of contact with volunteers who play with them and take care of them. Dogs, cats, pigs and other animals can live out their days in relative comfort. It's superior to confinement, but nowhere as good as having a home of one's own.

Bruce left for work, and I made more flyers. I called veterinarians'offices in the immediate neighborhood and beyond and asked them to be on the lookout for a dog resembling Marlena. I went to the housing projects and spoke to people sitting on benches outside. In the afternoon, when Ana came home, I told her what had happened. She quickly offered to help. She took a flyer to Staples and she ran off 100 copies. Together we papered the rest of the neighborhood. I returned to the shelter and checked the crates. On my way home, I approached a garbage truck and asked the sanitation workers if they looked for tags if they found a dead animal in the street. No, they didn't, one of the men told me. They just scooped them up. I handed him a flyer and asked that they keep an eye out for Marlena and call me if they found a carcass that resembled her.

Bruce was sure someone had taken her in, and I was sure she was dead. Suddenly, I burst into tears. When he tried to embrace me, I pushed him away. It was an odd moment. Years ago, when I had been visiting my parents in Florida and had received the terrible news about Mercury, I did need comfort. But my dad had turned and walked to the end of the living room and my mom didn't know what to do. It was probably a shock to them to see an adult cry, especially their own grown up daughter. Finally, my mom had put her arm around me, and patted my back, in a "there, there, now, everything is going to be all right" gesture. But it didn't make me feel any better.

Ana and I had taped flyers to lampposts in Central Park. The night Marlena took off, the doorman from the building on the next block said he thought he had seen a dog racing by. If Marlena had gone into the park, she'd be no more safe than if she were running through traffic. An off-leash dog might attack her. Raccoons posed another danger.

Leftover lunches filled the trash bins in every season, helping some of these critters to grow to the size of baby pigs. One could easily hurt Marlena.

Time moved slowly. When I tried to read a newspaper or sit down with a book, I felt edgy. I kept waiting for the phone to ring but the only sound in the building was that of construction workers, hammering and drilling. I had taken some flyers to the West Side, to a couple of pet supply stores within a few blocks of the park. They were not at all close to where we lived, but when I thought how far Max, the Rottweiler, had traveled the night he killed Monkey and Argo, I realized anything was possible.

Zorra sensed something was wrong. Instead of trying to get my husband or me to play with her by bringing a toy and bumping it into one of our legs, she lay on her cushion. Mozart, we had discovered, didn't play with toys, but he entertained us by dancing. When it was time to eat, he twirled around and around, sometimes so quickly that he lost his balance and fell. His mealtime antics were the only thing that made us smile during the days we searched for Marlena.

By Friday, I couldn't remain in the apartment any longer. Nothing was happening, and sitting around, experiencing the slow advancement of time, was making me crazy. A friend had called and asked if I wanted to play tennis in Central Park. Though it was late in the season, the weather had been unusually mild, and the courts had remained open. I said yes. A few weeks before, I had booked a private lesson at the club where I play on Roosevelt Island for that same day. If I played in the park, then had a workout with the tennis pro, I might be tired enough to sleep through the night.

When I returned from the park, the answering machine was blinking. It was probably my husband, calling to find out if I'd had any news of Marlena. I played the message.

"Hello, my name is Zita. I think I have your *Shipperke*. Please call me."

I grabbed a pen and wrote down the number. My heart was flying out of my chest. No matter that she had pronounced the breed's name with a "sh" sound instead of a hard "sk." I knew it was Marlena, It *had* to be. Zita told me that a strange little dog had strutted into the lobby of her friend Sarah's apartment building late Tuesday night. The concierge, knowing that Sarah had a cat, figured she was experienced with animals, and called her. She came down and took Marlena upstairs. The next day, Sarah called Zita, who agreed to stop by that evening, after work, and take a look at the dog. When Zita saw Marlena, she suspected she was microchipped. "This is a high class dog," she told Sarah.

The women knew a veterinarian who made house calls and had a scanner for reading microchips. All day Thursday, they tried to get in touch with him, but it turned out he was away on vacation. That's when Zita thought of checking with Animal Care and Control.

"Yes," the woman at the desk told her, "someone has been coming in and calling about a dog that matches the description of the animal you found." They gave Zita my phone number.

Still dressed in my tennis clothes, I grabbed the $500 reward money and headed towards the door. Then I remembered my lesson. It was with a world class instructor who charged accordingly, but I cancelled it. I knew I'd lose the money, but I didn't care. I was on my way to Marlena.

Chapter 26

Sister Sarah

Zita had told me her friend was a retired nun and that she lived on East 116th Street, between First Avenue and the East River. This was astonishing news. Marlena had traveled over a mile in the night, crossing six major avenues, dodging buses, trucks and cars, as well as deliverymen on bicycles, to end up safe, in the home of a nun. No question, this was a miracle. I hopped in a cab and raced to the address Zita had given me.

Sister Sarah White, a pert, gray-haired woman, welcomed me at her front door. I had phoned her right after Zita called, and she had assured me Marlena was doing just fine. In fact, she said, the dog had been curious about Lulu, her cat, and the two animals had sniffed each other in a friendly way. Sarah led me into the living room. Suddenly, I heard a growl, Marlena had been sleeping under a table, and she now stood up, and like a hungry lioness, slinked towards me.

"Marlena, it's me," I said. This was not the reception I'd anticipated. I sat down on the floor and called her again.

Still wary, she approached. All of a sudden, she caught my scent, and her whole demeanor changed. She jumped into my arms and licked my face, her little tongue flickering over my skin like a lizard's. In return, I scratched her behind the ears, although I knew she would have preferred a belly rub. Sarah had removed the bandages the night Marlena arrived. They'd come undone as she ran through the streets, trailing behind like a bridal veil. I told Sarah there was a reward, and even though she hadn't been aware of it, I shoved the money into her hand. "Give it to the church or keep it. But thank you for saving my dog."

I told her I wanted to get Marlena to the veterinarian right away, and that I'd be in touch. I called my husband, and later I left a message on Ana's machine. Amazingly, Marlena survived her night on the town with her stitches intact. The veterinarian changed the dressing and said to bring her back for suture removal in another few days. Everyone in his office smiled as we walked out the door, together.

Our dog family was whole once again, and this time, when I walked in the park, I told everybody about Marlena's adventure. Since it had a happy ending, it was easier to talk about than what had happened to Mercury, then Monkey and Argo. The people I spoke with said they hoped this marked the end of my troubles with Schipperkes. I said I hoped so, too.

Christmas approached, and I suggested to Bruce that we invite Zita and Sister Sarah to lunch at our apartment. The lobby hadn't been torn apart yet, so it still looked presentable, and on Sunday, there was no construction noise. We had bought a live tree, as we always did, and I decorated it with horse ornaments. I'd been collecting them for years, and had everything from a miniature needlepoint pillow my friend Sheena had made, to a white satin Pegasus I'd bought in Chinatown. Every year, until I told him to stop because the "barn" was too crowded, Bruce had added to the herd. Both Sarah and Zita were enchanted by my collection.

Bruce made one of his delicious bacon and cheese omelets. I poured the wine and we began to eat and chat. Sometime after the second glass of wine, Zita revealed that Sister Sarah was the granddaughter of a man who had designed mansions for the rich in New York City, during the Gilded Age, as well as the arch in Washington Square plus other landmarks. He was a dapper figure, and a pleasure-seeker, who threw lavish parties with endless Champagne. His life ended tragically at age 52, when the jealous husband of a young woman with whom he had had an affair years before, shot him at point blank range. He was the "White" of McKim, Meade and White, the prominent Beaux-Arts architectural firm, and his first name was Stanford. Sister Sarah never knew him, but she grew up on the family estate on Long Island. Hers was a childhood of dogs and horses and nannies to look after the children. It was thrilling for me to listen to her stories. She was a living connection to history.

Sarah often said that fate had brought Marlena to her doorstep that night. She told us the dog had entered the building and stood in the lobby as if she knew exactly where she was going. In subsequent visits, I took Marlena on the subway in the Sherpa® bag and walked the three blocks to Sarah's building. Marlena never overshot the entrance. She always headed straight to the door. Sarah, of course, became a special friend and we see each other to this day.

Chapter 27

Vietnam

Towards the middle of January, Bruce and I took another trip to Southeast Asia. This time we explored Vietnam with some of the same friends who had been on our previous trips, plus some newcomers. A few days before we left, I brought the dogs to the house. I had decided to try a new dog sitter, a young woman who ran a grooming and pet sitting service on Shelter Island. She'd agreed to spend the night at my place and to stop by during the day to let the dogs out and to feed them. I explained about our antiques and she promised to be careful. She had email at her place of business, and I wrote down the address. The hotels where we stayed always had Internet access, and this way, I could check from time to time to see how the "kids" were doing.

Once again, my husband entertained the other travelers with his cigar smoking and beer drinking. But on this trip, he found a buddy, a man named Howie. When a lid went "pop" on the bus, people could never be sure which man did it, and in most cases, the first "pop" was followed by a second. In Saigon, (Ho Chi Minh City), I found a department store with a display of the Eiffel Tower. It dominated at the entrance, just inside the lobby, and it was at least twenty feet high. This *Tour Eiffel* was constructed entirely of empty beer cans. I took a photo, and later, I found a street peddler selling baseball caps fashioned from empty cans of Tiger beer, a local brand Bruce favored. I bought one and surprised him later that evening. The next day, he wore it on the bus, eliciting chuckles from everyone, and jealous admiration from Howie.

No matter where we were in our travels, I always thought about the dogs. I thought how lucky they were to have us as "parents" compared to the poor, flea infested strays we saw in villages and cities throughout Southeast Asia. By the time we reached the last few days of our trip, I was anxious to get home, and to sleep in a bed, surrounded by dogs. Some people lock their dogs in the basement, or keep them in the garage, the kitchen, an outside dog house, or any place other than in the bedroom where, psychologically, a dog feels it's one of the pack. I never relegated any of our dogs to "Siberia." They always slept with us, snuggling between us, like Zorra, or on the pillow above my head, like Monkey, and then Marlena. Mo, like Argo, preferred to sleep on the floor in his own bed, which was always just a few feet away from ours. There was a time, eons ago, when I reached across the bedclothes to stroke my husband's bare skin as I awoke in the morning, but now, I loved touching a warm body covered with fur. I'm willing to bet, he did, too.

Chapter 28

Vivi

We arrived home in time for Westminster, and of course, I attended the show. The day after, Wednesday, the 15th, was my birthday, and when we came home from a fine dinner out, I heard heartbreaking news on the television. A Whippet, Ch. Bohem's C'est la Vie, call name Vivi, somehow had escaped from her crate as she was loading onto a plane at JFK airport. Like Argo, Vivi had won an Award of Merit at the Garden, and her owner, Jill, had just settled into her seat for the long flight home to California, when an attendant called her aside. With that, one of the biggest dog hunts in history began.

On one of my Internet dog lists, I learned of a search party that had been organized to canvass the airport hangars and cargo areas over the weekend in hopes of finding some trace of Vivi. The weather that week was frigid, with temperatures in the low teens, and the wind blew close to gale force. Normally, on such a winter weekend, Bruce and I might bundle up, go to a movie, and drop into a restaurant for a long lunch of oysters and wine. But that Saturday, a feeling in my gut told me I had to help find this dog.

A group of dog lovers, mostly women, had gathered outside Terminal C in the cargo area at JFK Airport. One had driven down from Connecticut, and others had come from different parts of the region, Long Island, New Jersey, and the city. We looked like a bunch of Mt. Everest climbers, encased in our down coats and scarves, but even so, the wind delivered teeth-chattering cold to our bodies. It was hard to imagine that a skinny Whippet could have survived the night under these conditions. Delta, the airline whose inept handling of the dog's

IN THE SHADOW OF MERCURY

crate had resulted in this tragedy, and the Port Authority of New York and New Jersey had conducted their own search of the airport since the escape, and the story was all over the television news and the tabloids. Yet nobody had spotted the dog.

Bonnie, the search coordinator, had made a batch of "lost dog" flyers. Like a military tactician, she divided us into teams of two and dispatched us to canvass the cargo area and give a flyer to any employees we might meet, asking them to keep an eye out for Vivi. I remember going into one warehouse-sized building, walking around, calling out to see if anyone was around, then wandering past machinery bays, still without seeing a soul. It amazed me that there was no security guard to challenge me. I taped a flyer to the wall and left.

My partner and I then cruised the neighborhood adjacent to the airport, stopping at gas stations to hand out flyers, and speaking to people on the street. Since I had experience approaching strangers from my search for Marlena, I didn't mind getting out of the car with a flyer and going up to a stone-faced guy walking a Pit Bull, for example. It amazed me, that with all the media attention, there still were people who weren't aware of Vivi's misfortune. Meanwhile, other volunteers were doing the same thing in different sections of the neighborhood. By mid-afternoon, my toes had grown numb and I decided to go home. Before leaving, I put myself on the email list for further search assignments. For several weeks, I helped look for Vivi. Bonnie had chopped up the borough of Queens into sectors, dispatching volunteers, armed with flyers, translated into Russian, Chinese, Korean, and Spanish, to every area where a sighting of a Whippet had been reported. And there had been sightings. As incredible as it seemed, the dog appeared to have left the airport and skidaddled towards residential neighborhoods near Crocheron Park, in Flushing.

One weekend, Jill and Rick, Vivi's owners, and her handler, Bo, flew in from California to help search. Perhaps the dog would pick up their scent, or hear them calling her, and come out from her hiding place. At that time, everyone was convinced she'd be found. But the weeks became months, and the sightings became fewer, until there were none at all. A year passed, and then another, marking the sad anniversaries of Vivi's disappearance. A few die-hard people kept looking, posting flyers and scouring neighborhoods. But the official search had come to a close.

Chapter 29

The Hunt

In March, I began looking for a new apartment. The dust and noise from the demolition made normal living impossible. Even Bruce agreed that we had to move. This surprised me. He'd been in that apartment since 1969, years before we ever met. He wasn't a person who welcomed change. To move things along, I agreed to do the legwork, visiting apartments and bringing him only to the ones I liked. This was tricky. He was still working in New Jersey, and most co-ops didn't allow real estate brokers and their clients in for visits after 6 p.m. during the week. In many buildings, weekends were off-limits as well. We had decided, reluctantly, that we'd have to buy an apartment. It didn't make sense financially, at our respective ages. But there were few, if any, rentals in the area I'd specified—86th to 96th Street, between Park Avenue and Fifth. With three dogs, it was important to live near Central Park.

For thirty years, I'd lived in an apartment I'd always considered too small. What an eye opener it was, then, to visit other two-bedroom, two-bath residences whose rooms were the same size as ours, or smaller. For two million dollars, I could enjoy less space than I had but pay more for it. One building I visited made the broker wait outside on the street, instead of letting her sit on a sofa in the lobby. I found that weird, especially since she looked and dressed as though she lived there—cashmere wrap, pearls, ballerina flats, and a good handbag. I didn't care for the apartment she showed me, which was just as well, since I probably wouldn't have liked the snoots that lived there, and they probably wouldn't have approved us as shareholders.

Another building, on Park Avenue at 88th Street, had two apartments for sale, and for these I called my husband. Here the rooms were large, with enormously high ceilings and huge walk in closets that could serve as guest bedrooms if inflatable beds were placed on the floor. I noticed Bruce calculating how many cubic feet of space he'd have for stacking his old newspapers. I knew he liked these apartments, but ultimately, I told him, no. They were in the back of the building, literally half a block from the front door. This meant that Marlena and Mozart, the two oldest dogs, would have a distance to travel in the morning until they reached the pavement for relief. In addition, Park Avenue was further away from Central Park, one long block to be exact. While that might not seem like a big deal to non-doggy people, I figured it would add an extra twenty minutes to my round-trip morning walk. Dogs, after all, don't move in a straight line. They like to stop and sniff trees, dumpsters, and bags of trash piled on the sidewalks. I told the broker not to show me any more listings on Park.

A well-priced apartment, facing Central Park, sounded almost perfect when the broker described it. The "almost" was the location—Fifth Avenue at 108th Street. This was around the block from the corner where we had encountered the glowering young men the night Marlena took off. The nearest subway stop was on Lexington Avenue at 110th Street, a station where I, as a middle-aged white woman, would only feel safe walking home towards Fifth Avenue during the day. The broker and I arrived around eleven a.m., and had to make throat clearing noises to awaken the concierge who had dozed off at her desk in the lobby. She smiled, clearly embarrassed, signed us in, then waved us towards the elevator. This apartment did, indeed, face the park, but it was on the second floor, so there was no panorama, only tree limbs. The rooms were about the same size as my apartment, but there were two more of them. Even so, I wasn't interested. I re-emphasized that 96th Street was my northern boundary.

Real estate brokers always try to sneak in something they hope will be tempting. Mine convinced me to check out a co-op on the corner of 98th Street and Fifth, adjacent to Mt. Sinai Hospital. Though the apartment itself was acceptable, the location was not. Ambulances zoomed around the corner. There was no place to park or double park to unload the car when returning from Shelter Island. The street was too narrow and clogged with hospital traffic. A building on 97th Street and Fifth was also out of the question. On that street, there was no stopping or standing permitted for most of the day since it was the route traffic took to go west, through the park. I had also told the broker that I didn't want to see anything that needed work. We were, after all, fleeing a construction zone, so it was important to find a place that had already been updated and renovated. This narrowed the selection significantly.

Chapter 30

Reunion

In April, I took a break from apartment hunting and flew to the west coast with Marlena. Bruce had offered me a slew of his miles and I was able to get a free First Class round-trip ticket. Perversely, I had to pay for Marlena. At least there was more room for her Sherpa® bag under the seat than in coach. We were headed to Vancouver, Washington for the Schipperke Club of America's National Specialty. This was another all-Schipperke event, with conformation classes ranging from Puppies to Veterans, plus Obedience. I'd entered Marlena in Veterans, a designation for dogs and bitches eight years or older. Ruth, her breeder, was going to be there, and I thought it would be fun to get the "girls" together again. By pre-arrangement, I met Ruth in the hospitality suite at the hotel where we all were staying. She had told me on the phone how excited she felt about seeing Marlena again. But Marlena walked right past her.

"Marlena, it's Ruth," I said. But Marlena had gotten a whiff of the food on the table and her little nose was pointed skyward, sucking in the aromas and wondering, I was sure, how she might grab a snack. Finally, I got her attention, and she let Ruth pet her.

When it came time for the Veterans class, I chickened out. Here were all these Schipperke breeders, including Krista, who handled their own entries, and who were active in the show world throughout the year. They were experts, and I was a bumbler. For several weeks before this trip, I had practiced at home with Marlena, and in fact, I had showed her once back in the fall. The Queensboro Kennel Club offered a Veterans class, and I had entered her there. She easily won Best in Breed in Veterans. She was the only Schipperke entry. Even my handling couldn't take that away from her. But when it came to Best Veteran, we were outclassed. In fact, I remember the winner. A big, male Bull Terrier, whom I thought was too heavy and clunky. What did I know? He was Rufus, (Ch. Rocky Top's Sundance Kid) who went on to win Westminster that year. In any event, going Best of Breed entitled me to have my picture taken with my prize winning bitch and the judge. I had worn a red coat that day, creating a perfect background for the photo. I framed one shot for the mantel in the living room and sent the other to Ruth.

When Marlena's former handler approached me at the Specialty, and offered to show her for me in Veterans, I exhaled with relief. Though Marlena didn't win any ribbons that day, she sure looked good.

Chapter 31

10128

In June, I found the perfect apartment. It was in a building that reminded me of a small Parisian hotel. I had walked past it many times during the years I lived a few blocks further uptown. I always admired the window boxes, painted dark green, and planted with dwarf pine trees whose needles perfectly matched the vessels in which they grew. From the street, the black and white marble entryway spoke of earlier and elegant times. The location, too, was outstanding. A few feet west of the building stood a fire hydrant, an easy spot to tuck into for unloading a car full of dogs. Number nine, which was the address, had the good fortune of being located on the quietest section of East 96th Street. As mentioned earlier, 96th Street crosstown traffic jogged north for one block on Madison, then turned west on 97th to traverse the park. Across from "Nine" on the south side of the street, cars, buses, and trucks exited the park, traveling east and often causing congestion, but 96th Street on the north side was almost as serene as a cul-de-sac. The building was half a block from the park and it had a classier zip code, 10128.

The apartment had been totally updated with a state-of-the art kitchen, including all the big name, trendy appliances. They looked modern and sleek, but I couldn't have cared less because I don't do much cooking, yet it seemed fun to have the latest stove, dishwasher and refrigerator without the annoyance of having had to go out and shop for them or pay a decorator to do it. The couple selling the apartment, a pair of young lawyers, had taken all the "how-to-sell-your-apartment" tips to heart. There were no newspapers stacked on the coffee table, only glossy architectural magazines, and the closets, though much smaller than the ones on Park Avenue, contained fewer clothes, making them seem more spacious than they were in reality. The apartment boasted a washer/dryer, an amenity coveted by New Yorkers, and something I grew to appreciate since I could take care of my tennis gear right after a match. And it had a dining room. On Shelter Island, the dining room was my favorite place in the house, but our New York apartment didn't have one. Instead, we'd put a table and chairs at one end of the living room, creating a dining area. It worked, but having a separate room was better. It provided more space for our armoire and hutch, two French country pieces we'd bought years before when such antiques were affordable.

The living room faced 96th Street, with views into the apartments on the other side, but it was the bedroom that sold me on this co-op. Next to this building was a low-rise, landmark townhouse, used as a school. So, from the bedroom, on the 12th floor, one could see the Central Park reservoir as well as the El Dorado apartment building, on Central Park West, with its majestic towers silhouetted against the setting sun. Gulls and pigeons swooped over the treetops, and in the months before the Claremont Riding Academy closed, horseback riders, cantering on the bridle path, could also be seen from this window. The apartment was everything I wanted but thought I could never find.

Bruce came to look, and though he said the apartment was acceptable, I knew he was comparing it to the ones we'd seen on Park Avenue. This was smaller in room size, yet more expensive. He worried that his hulking desk might not fit through the doorway, and around the turns of the hall that led to the second bedroom which would serve as his office. But even worse, he realized he'd have to say bye-bye to a good part of his old newspaper collection. This pleased me as I pictured a home free of eyesores, a neat, tidy habitat, not exactly magazine-spread perfect, but close to it.

I wanted this apartment. I explained to him that in all my searching, this was the only one with the best location, no need for additional work, not even a paint job, and a terrific view from the master bedroom. Ninety-sixth Street was as broad as a boulevard, so it didn't matter, at least to me, that other people's living rooms were across the way. In addition, it was a pet friendly building. I'd already seen a Bernese Mountain Dog and a Pug going out for a walk. I told Bruce not to dither, to pay the asking price and to do it soon. A gem like this was not going to stay long on the market.

In a few weeks, I planned to leave for Shelter Island. I had arranged with Ana for us to take Lucy for the summer. The old dog deserved a couple of months in the country plus a reunion with her buddy, Zorra.

That meant we needed to move quickly with the apartment. Bruce returned a few times with his measuring tape. This was a good sign, but each time he bent down to check on the outlets or to assess where a piece of furniture might fit, I feared some other person was on the phone at that very moment, telling his or her broker, "I'll take it."

Several days of measuring and pondering passed, but finally my husband relented. Now it was a question of meeting with the co-op board. As it turned out, we both felt we were being interviewed by our adult children, if we had had any. The three young men who met with us were all under forty. We liked them. They liked us. And I suppose our financials made their eyes gleam. We intended to pay cash for the unit.

The closing was set for August, and in the meantime, I took off for the island. Four dogs, I figured, were as easy to handle as three, especially since we had an acre and a half of our property fenced in for them to roam. But Marlena, Zorra and Mozart enjoyed a leashed walk with me every morning, and the first time I tried to take Lucy with us, I realized it wasn't going to work. Lucy still was obese, and her stumpy legs couldn't carry her more than a few hundred feet before she started panting and looking at me with eyes that said, "Can't I please go home?"

So, I brought her back to the house, put her in the sun porch, and set off again with my dogs. When we returned, about half an hour later, Lucy was standing in the yard. I opened the gate, then let my dogs off the leash and watched them race up the hill. When Lucy lumbered up to me, I gave her a big pat. But then I saw the screens. She had chewed holes in two of them, and then, like a rampaging rhinoceros, bulldozed her way out, denting the metal frames as she plunged to freedom. I couldn't yell at her. Clearly, she had been so anxious about being left behind, she did what her doggy brain thought was best, and that was, catch up with the pack at all costs.

After that, I took my morning walk in shifts. I always left one of the Schips or Zorra with Lucy, then returned to take another walk with the dog that had been baby-sitting. This worked fine for the dogs, but it ate up more of my morning that I would have liked. Even though I got up at 5:30 or 6, I had a few chores to attend to before the walk—let the dogs out, pick up the poop, feed them, get my own breakfast, then read the papers left over from the day before. On the island, the current day's papers didn't arrive much before 8:30 a.m. and by then, I was preparing for my next activity. Often, I had tennis matches starting at 9 a.m., and before Lucy arrived, I never had to rush to be ready. But with the extra walking required to keep her from tearing down my house, I had to scramble to get geared up and arrive at the courts on time.

The rest of the summer passed uneventfully. I had planned for Lucy to sleep in the sun porch, on a cozy, fleece covered bed, but somehow, the first night, she waddled upstairs, and after that, she slept in the bedroom with the rest of the dogs. I was always a bit nervous in the morning when she trundled down. My stairs are wood, and don't offer any traction. One slip and her weight could have sent her spiraling to the bottom. I made sure to walk in front of her, as a buffer, in case she needed help.

My husband liked Lucy, too. But he was amazed at her girth. I had cut down on her food and she lost a pound or two, but it didn't show. At the vet's, she weighed in at 65, and normally, a dog like her should weigh 40 to 45 pounds. I suggested to Ana that she put Lucy on a diet, so by the following summer, the dog wouldn't be as heavy. I had offered, and Ana had accepted, that as long as Lucy lived, she could spend the summers with us.

In August, we closed on the apartment. The dogs hadn't seen their new home, but I knew they'd be happy there. I pictured them trotting from room to room, sniffing every corner, delighted at the expanded indoor space suddenly available to them. Bruce continued to measure and to grumble about the small closets, but occasionally, I caught him smiling.

We moved on September 13th. For some people, that might have been an ominous date, a day to stay home and avoid new activities. But for me—for us—it held promise. It was the promise of new beginnings.

The End